# WHY WORSHIP GOD?
(when He hasn't been so nice to me)

MATT OPPENHEIM

Why Worship God?

(when He hasn't been so nice to me)

Publisher: Cosmic Publishing

© 2011 Matt Oppenheim. All rights reserved. Reproduction of any part of this work beyond that permitted by Section 107 or 108 of the 1976 United States Copyright Act without the express written permission of the copyright owner is unlawful. Requests for permission or further information should be addressed to the author.

Unless otherwise indicated, Scripture quotations used in the book are from the Holy Bible, New International Version, copyright © 1973, 1978, 1984 by International Bible Society.

Cover art by Don Wilson

Set in Palatino Linotype

ISBN-13: 978-0-6154-8822-6 (Cosmic Publishing)

ISBN-10: 0-6154-8822-6

# Contents

Introduction..........1

1. Why Does the World Suck So Bad?..........11
   *Free Will*
   *The Fall of Man, or Original Sin*
   *Satan is Alive and Well*
   *We are Free to Choose Jesus…or Not*
   *God is Always with Us*

2. Change..........29

3. The Holy Spirit..........37

4. A World Without God..........43

5. The Hope Exchange..........53

6. God's Gifts for Us All..........63
   *We All Have Gifts*
   *Community*
   *A Government Created by God*
   *A Savior for Everyone*

7. The Gift of Earth..........73

8. The Comparison Dilemma..........85
   *The House in the Desert*

| | | |
|---|---|---|
| 9 | The Gift of Jesus..........99 | |
| | *Degrees of Sin* | |
| | *Chip* | |
| | *The Ladder* | |

| | | |
|---|---|---|
| 10 | Heaven's Boot Camp..........121 | |
| | *Twenty-four Years of Problems* | |
| | *Problems Affect Everyone* | |
| | *Problems Aren't Necessarily Punishment* | |
| | *Problems Help Us Grow* | |
| | *The Problem Transfer* | |

| | | |
|---|---|---|
| 11 | Not to Worry..........139 | |

| | | |
|---|---|---|
| 12 | Called Up to the Big Leagues...........147 | |
| | *The Story of Johnny and Josh* | |
| | *The Blackout* | |
| | *The Marble Jar* | |

| | | |
|---|---|---|
| 13 | God's Plan was Bigger than Mine..........165 | |
| | *My Divine Business Partner* | |
| | *Aunt Nellie and the GPS* | |

| | | |
|---|---|---|
| 14 | Finale..........177 | |
| | *My Software Parable* | |
| | *What's the Worst Thing that can Happen?* | |

Notes..........187

# Acknowledgments

- *To my wife, Kim.* You are the best…wife, mother, friend, advisor. You shoot me straight when I need it, and shoot me straight when I don't need it. You are my cheerleader, critic and number one supporter. I'm going to request a contract extension in April.

- *To my girls, Maddie and Emma.* Thanks for all the material that you didn't even know you provided, and thanks for being, well, kids.

- *To Craig, Eli, and Rufus, my favorite pastors.* Your relevant approach to Christianity made me realize that Jesus is approachable, and He wants to hang out with me everywhere and everyday. Some of your advice was too good to be left out of this book. I know; you don't like to take credit for God's work. So I thank God for you guys.

- *To my parents, Don and Kathy*, for laying a foundation of Christianity that I walked away from, and came back to. Faith comes so much easier when it is woven into the soul at birth.

- ❖ ***To Kim's parents, Don and Rosemary.*** You guys redefine support; you are always there to back me up, regardless of my crazy idea. You gave Kim her Christian roots, and it's easy to see where she gets her encouraging demeanor!

- ❖ ***To our Small Bible Study Group.*** When our little group started five years ago, it was my hope that we could see our kids grow up together. That is happening with every passing Bible study, church service, dinner or event, and I am grateful. I couldn't think of any other group of people to share my imperfect life with. Jill D and John Z…thank you for the edits!

- ❖ ***Last but not least, to Jesus.*** I am grateful to be your servant; that you would use my brain and fingertips to peck out a book that glorifies You. It is my prayer that this book will speak biblical truths, and be an encouragement to anyone who may be beaten down by life. Thank you for loving us, and I can't wait to meet you face-to-face one day!

# Introduction

I'm a classic rock guy. Which is a little strange to write, since I've been on a country kick for the past two years. Which is even stranger to write, because when I was on my classic rock phase I never would have dreamed of listening to country. In fact, we were the guys that beat up the country fans. Since my classic rock roots, I've been through pop, alternative, blue grass, alt-country, grunge, jam bands, even a little hip-hop. But I always go back to the classic rock.

As a child of the eighties, I had a much greater appreciation for bands like Led Zeppelin and The Who than I did for Michael Jackson. I knew all the band members names, and bought all of their albums.

I know Kenney Jones replaced the late Keith Moon as The Who's drummer after he died in '78. I also know that in reality, Keith Moon could never be replaced.

I know that Neil Peart is the new guy in Rush, even though

# WHY WORSHIP GOD?

he's been with the band since 1974. This is because he wasn't the drummer on the band's first album.

I am the guy who knows that Eddie Van Halen actually got drums for Christmas, and his brother Alex got the guitar.

I know if you play "Stairway to Heaven" backwards, it really does sound creepy, but I think it's a coincidence. We were able to play songs backwards back then by rotating the turntable backwards. How do they do it today?

When I look at my teenager today—aside from the devices that play back music—not much has changed. She is just as much into her music as I was into mine. She owns the music magazines, wears the concert tees, and hangs her favorite band's posters on her wall, just like I did. Music has the ability to transport you to a different state of being. It can make a bad day better and a good day great. I guess that's why its power hasn't faded with the generations.

I could go on and on about classic rock. I put a lot of time into my music back then, studying those bands and listening to all those great songs. I put so much effort into my appreciation for music; I guess you could say I *worshiped* a lot of those bands. If Robert Plant told me to go rob a bank, I probably would have done it.

I put much more time into rock n' roll than I put into my church, that's for sure. Who can blame me? I mean, rock music is fun. And church? Well, church is a drag. When I was in high school, church was a parental requirement, while rock n' roll was an obsession.

## Introduction

Worship doesn't stop at music, either. Actors, athletes and other celebrities have a great influence—not just over our youth—but all of us. We buy tee-shirts, DVDs, books, posters, magazines. All these things are the equivalent of worship on some level.

Growing up, we are told to go to church and worship God. If I could have so much enthusiasm toward my rock and roll heroes, how come I didn't have that kind of appreciation for the Creator of the universe?

I think there are a couple of obvious reasons for this. First, my music heroes were all about the good times. Same thing with the other celebrities, too. To see a rockin' concert, watch a pro ball game or a great movie—we associate all these activities with the joyful moments in life. God, on the other hand, is more about rules. He represents the wet towel of life. God wants us to obey our parents, not to swear, not to go all the way before marriage, not to drink too much. Who would want to worship that? That's no fun, right?

My other observation is that my favorite celebrities aren't here to discipline me. In fact, they don't have any personal contact with me at all. The Rolling Stones could care less about what I do on Friday night. But God does. God has a purpose for our lives, so how we act matters very much to Him. Because of this, we will all experience some painful lessons in life. Why would we want to worship a God that puts us through pain?

As we grow into adults, it is impossible to overlook the trouble in this world. War, natural disasters, impoverished nations, terminal illness…these things seem to dominate a society in a world created by God. How could He let these things happen, over and over and over again? Trials don't just occur on a global level, either. Don't we all get beaten down by life sometimes?

After I got married, my wife and I both agreed that we would raise our family in a Christian home. After a five-year hiatus, I started going to church again. When I returned to church after all those years, I'm what you might call the bitter Christian. I sat in the service, listening to how great our God was. I saw the people around me praising God—showing what appeared to be heartfelt worship—and there I was with my hands in my pockets. I just didn't get it. I've had a crummy week. I've had a crummy year. So-and-so has cancer. So-and-so just got laid off, and he has a wife and three kids to feed. I wanted to tap the worshipers next to me and ask, "Haven't you read the news lately? This world sucks, and you guys are praising the One who made it that way."

To keep the peace in my new marriage, I kept going. Isn't that what you're supposed to do? Just go, keep your mouth shut and deal with it for an hour a week.

But God doesn't want you go through the motions. He resents half-hearted worship. Revelation Chapter 3 reads, *"I know your deeds, that you are neither cold nor hot. I wish you were either one or the other! So, because you are lukewarm—neither hot nor cold—I am about to spit you out of my mouth."*[1]

Wow. I didn't know this verse at the time. But I didn't have to. One day I decided that I didn't want to be lukewarm; I didn't

## Introduction

want church to be a marital obligation anymore. I wanted my Christianity to burn like a fire. I made the decision to learn more about God and find out for myself what was wrong with my attitude.

That decision is what led to this book. In a sense, I wrote this book for selfish reasons. I had to find out what was missing in my perception of God. If there were so many people in that church each week being moved by the Holy Spirit, I had to learn more.

I'm so glad I did.

All of this happened about eight years ago. That's when, after thirty-five years, I started to get to *know* God instead of know *about* Him. A relationship; not shackled by a denomination—all Christian denominations acknowledge Jesus as the Son of God and the Savior—but a relationship with God through Jesus. Reading His word, talking to Him daily in prayer. Figuring out His yes' from His no's. Just like getting to know a friend. And listen, I'm not there yet. Not hardly. I will spend the rest of my life getting to know Jesus, and that relationship will continue after I leave this earth.

One of the first things I set out to do is redefine the term "worship" as it relates to God. I always thought of worship as being mesmerized at a concert by your favorite band, or maybe how in high school many of us had "hero worship" for someone we wanted to be like. That's not really what I'm talking about here; that's more infatuation than worship. The word worship is derived from the Old English word "worthscipe," meaning

# WHY WORSHIP GOD?

worthiness or worth-ship. When we hear of God being worthy, we are giving Him credit for all creation. We are saying He is the only one worthy of being called Master of the Universe. That's easy enough. After all, it is His universe. I can give Him credit for that. When we acknowledge this, we need to remember His gifts to us and be thankful for them. C'mon, you can think of one good thing about your life, right? Well, start there, and be thankful to God for it.

What does God say about worship? Look at the fourth commandment, *"Remember to keep the Sabbath holy."*[2] This not only commands you to worship, but to observe a day of rest as well.

In the second book of Kings, God makes it clear: *"But the LORD, who brought you up out of Egypt with mighty power and outstretched arm, is the one you must worship. To him you shall bow down and to him offer sacrifices. Do not worship other gods. Do not forget the covenant I have made with you, and do not worship other gods. Rather, worship the LORD your God; it is he who will deliver you from the hand of all your enemies."*[3]

And Psalm 150: *Praise the LORD.*

*Praise God in his sanctuary; praise him in his mighty heavens. Praise him for his acts of power; praise him for his surpassing greatness. Praise him with the sounding of the trumpet, praise him with the harp and lyre, praise him with timbrel and dancing, praise him with the strings and pipe, praise him with the clash of cymbals, praise him with resounding cymbals.*

*Let everything that has breath praise the LORD.*

# Introduction

*Praise the LORD.*[4]

How do we acknowledge this? There are lots of ways to worship. Going to church, reading the Bible or Christian books, singing, praying, helping those less fortunate, meditation, observing religious holidays, giving, or tithing are all forms of worship.

Worship doesn't have to be loud or animated like a concert. The church services I attend are a little more solemn, somewhat quieter than your average concert. In essence, I shouldn't feel bad if I don't flail my arms around in church. Good flailing doesn't necessarily equal good worship. Believing God is the Divine Master, Ruler and Creator in your heart is the foundation of good worship.

But having a better understanding of the concept of worship doesn't make the world any better. It didn't make my boss any less of a jerk this week.

That's how I used to think, until I realized that God and His role in our lives is misunderstood. I think there are a lot of people out there who are mad at God, or at least don't believe He can impact their daily lives. A lot of us here are expecting perfection. Well, earth is not the perfect place, heaven is. So, if you're seeking perfection on this planet, you are going to be disappointed. And when we get disappointed, we blame God. How can God let this happen, or that happen? The truth is, we live in an imperfect world where a perfect God has given us the freedom to make our own decisions. When you take this freedom and couple it with the sin nature we inherited from

# WHY WORSHIP GOD?

Adam and Eve, terrible things can happen. But, this is not God's fault. He is only giving us the freedom we asked for.

Not too long ago I read a blog entitled, "How could a loving God let crack babies be born?" I'll tell you why: Because the mother of the crack baby made the wrong choice. It was the mother of the child that caused this, not God. You could just as easily ask, "How could a loving mother let her son play football, knowing that he is going to get his block knocked off?" I guess this means that the mother doesn't love her son if she's going to subject him to such brutality, right? We both know this couldn't be further from the truth. The mother lets him play because it is his desire, and she loves him enough to let him try. It's the child's choice to play football; the mother is simply honoring his wishes. Is she going to worry about him on that field? Absolutely.

God loves us, too. He loves us enough to let make our own decisions.

When our choices—or the choices of others—cause pain in our lives, God is the one being in the universe that can help us through them. Do you see where I'm headed with this? God is not necessarily the cause of our problems…He is the solution! That's why it is so important not to push God away when troubles come, but rather to bring Him closer. And that can be a hard thing to do. Especially if you're leaving behind a loved one at the cemetery, walking out of a divorce attorney's office, or leaving a doctors office with a life changing diagnosis. It can be very hard to do. But it's a fact: We grow the most in our faith

## Introduction

during the difficult times. God will get you through them.

I would like you to meet the cast of characters in this book. You got, well, me. I have to tell you, I'm not a preacher or a seminary student. In fact, I sell insurance for a living. After going through this seven-year journey, I felt a burning desire to share with you what I've learned; that you and God are actually on the same side of life's problems. My wife Kim; I mention her quite a bit. And my two daughters, Maddie, who is thirteen, and Emma, who is five. You will find many little anecdotes about my family in these pages.

For anyone who attends Hope Church in Cordova, Tennessee, you may also hear the echoes of our pastors. I thank God for giving Craig and Eli the charisma and personality to communicate His word in such a provoking, applicable, and many times humorous way. It is God's work though this church and its leadership that was a catalyst for this little book.

So here goes. Come along with me in these pages and discover what I learned about our God. He's not out to get us after all! He is a God who loves, protects, nurtures and corrects. He provides for us in so many ways that most of the time we don't realize it, or we just take it for granted.

If you are like I was—a little beat down by the world—and a little confused as to why you should go to church on Sunday, then I pray that I might be able to show you God from a different perspective. I can now say that I can worship God with sincere thanks and gratitude, and I now see God and this world much differently, and it's my prayer that this book may help you discover it too. Finally, I pray that this book will speak biblical truths and glorify God.

# Chapter 1:
# Why Does the World Suck So Bad?

Dear Claims Department:

Please accept this letter as a notice of intent to file a claim on my homeowners insurance policy. I feel a little explanation is in order.

As you may be aware, the city cut off the water main on the east side of our town on Thursday, August 30th to replace a pipe in the sewer line. I received a letter from the city stating the work would take about four hours to complete. With Labor Day weekend starting on Friday, my family and I made the decision to go spend a few days at my in-laws. This way we could avoid the temporary water shortage all

# WHY WORSHIP GOD?

together.

The letter from the city advised that we close all our drains to prevent any sewer gases from escaping into our house while the repairs were being conducted, which I did. After my wife scolded our son for bringing a frog in the house, we hopped in the car (no pun intended) and left for the weekend.

The following morning I received a call from our neighbor, stating that our water hose had been running, apparently all night. He told me he turned off the spigot. I must admit, I was a little confused as to how this happened, but aside from a little higher water bill, I didn't feel like any real harm was done.

Early Friday afternoon, the same neighbor called, explaining that he had come home for lunch, and the water on the driveway still had not dried. With the temperature in the 90s—and no rain—he thought it strange that the driveway would still be wet five hours after turning off the spigot. That's when he noticed that the water was actually coming from under the garage door. Upon further investigation, he reported that water was also coming from the front and back doors as well.

Somewhat panicked at this point, I told my neighbor where we hide the spare key to our house. When he opened the door, he was greeted by a flood of

## Why Does the World Suck so Bad?

water, which completely drenched his Italian loafers. Upon entering, he saw the kitchen faucet running full blast. After turning it off, he still heard water running. In going through the house, he found that every faucet in the house had been running. My guess is every faucet in the house had been running for about twenty-four hours, including one bathtub.

Our house is destroyed. The carpet is completely saturated. It smells like a wet dog. The sofa smells like a wet dog. Our dog smells like a wet dog. There is a six-inch water line on all our walls; below that line, you can poke a hole in the drywall with your finger. All the light fixtures survived unharmed, however. So did the doorknobs and house plants.

As you can imagine, we were all perplexed as to how this could have happened. Until we spoke to our child.

On that Thursday morning, as my wife and I were packing the car, our seven year-old son befriended a large toad in our front yard. Mr. or Ms. Claims Person, I do not know about your own personal history as a frog-handler. If you have no prior toad experience, I should tell you that they tend to leak when you hold them. I am not really sure where this leakage comes from, and in this context it is probably not necessary to expand on any theories.

# WHY WORSHIP GOD?

Unbeknownst to us, our son felt like it would be prudent to wash his hands of all toad juice before leaving for MawMaws. Apparently, when the outside hose didn't work, Ben entered the house to try our kitchen faucet, then the bathroom faucet, then the other bathroom faucet, and so on. I admire his tenacity, because he tried every faucet in the house, including the bathtub, only to find that none of them worked.

When my son attempted to wash the frog juice from his hands—and none of the faucets worked—he apparently didn't see any real need in turning each one back to its closed position. This lead to the realization that if a closed drain prevents gas from leaking *up* into the house, it makes sense that it would prevent water from going *down* into the drainpipe as well. When the city turned the water back on, and all our drains in were closed, the water really had no where to go except over the edge of the sink or tub, and onto our floor. This is where it accumulated to a level high enough to ruin my neighbor's shoes.

As of this date, we have captured at least six frogs, and have yet to positively identify the one who caused this mess. Please rest assured that we won't stop until we find this villain.

We are in the process of securing bids on the

```
rebuilding of our house.  I will forward to you once
I receive.  Thank you for your consideration in this
matter.
```

## Why Does the World Suck so Bad?

The above letter is fictitious, but I would not be surprised in the least if it really happened to me. Most of us have encountered an infuriating catastrophe like this at one time or another. Why do things like this have to happen?

The world is full of problems...even unbelievably ridiculous problems like the one in my imaginary letter. And these problems can be as close to home as an overflowing sink, or across the world. I would venture to say that a day *without* problems is more the exception than the rule. Wouldn't you agree? And our problems can be far more devastating than a flooded house. This earth is filled with sickness, disasters, war, and a lot of not-so-nice people. From hurricanes and earthquakes—to violent crime and acts of terrorism—to the accident that is preventing you from getting home after work, there is no where you can turn where you won't hear of a story that is disturbing at some level.

And then there is God. The God of the universe, the Almighty, the only one who has the power to stop or prevent this awful stuff from happening. He just sits in heaven watching while the world crumbles around us, like a superhero in hiding.

How could He do this to us? I thought our God was a God of

love, and that He wants to nurture and protect His children? Furthermore, why would I want to worship a God who has put me in this horrible world and allowed such horrible things to happen?

When someone asks questions like these, my first reaction is to figure out where they got the idea that the world was perfect. The world is full of imperfect people, resulting in an imperfect world. Jesus himself even said, *"In this world you WILL have trouble."*[1] Problems are guaranteed. It kills me when I hear people say, "I tried going to church, but it didn't make my problems go away, so I quit going."

I always thought the perfect place was heaven. People get confused by how a perfect God could create an imperfect world.

When Emma was four, we took a trip to Disney World. This trip was special in that it was her first trip to Disney, as well as mine—at age 41. A month or so after the trip, Emma and I were looking at some of the pictures from our adventure. Emma talked about how much fun it was, and why we couldn't just live at Disney World. I explained to her if we lived there, and could be there everyday, it wouldn't be as special to us anymore. One of the things that makes a place like Disney so magical is the fact that we can only go a few times in our life. If we were roommates with Mickey, we would very quickly take him for granted.

Don't you think the same can be said about heaven and earth? If earth were perfect, there wouldn't be a need for heaven. In this regard, it is the imperfection of our current life that gives us hope

## Why Does the World Suck so Bad?

for our afterlife. We all possess an innate craving to be with God, and that craving won't be satisfied until we are in heaven with him. In the meantime, we are stuck down here with traffic jams and stock market crashes.

In this chapter, we will discuss three concepts which may help you understand how we arrived at the world we have today.

**Free Will**

On that same trip to Disney World, we happened to be there the same week as the premier of the movie "*Up.*" *Up* was an animated feature about an old guy who launches his house with a billion balloons and goes on the adventure he always wanted to have…but that's not the point. The point is they built an exhibit that illustrated how the characters were created. To the inner geek in me, this was fascinating. The exhibit had the original sketches of the characters, then sort of a chronology of how they evolved into the final versions which appeared in the film. It also included some concepts they didn't go with. It was amazing to see the countless drawings the creators made to finally arrive at the characters who starred in the movie.

Think of the process God went through when he created man. The Bible says we are created in His own image, but God didn't have to make us that way. He could have made us look any way he wanted. Remember Yoda from Star Wars? That could be a human. An octopus? Sure, that could be us. Really, God created us from a blank sheet of paper, and He is responsible for our design. When I think of that exhibit at Disney, I can't help but think of God sitting behind this divine drawing table with all these different sketches of what humans could have looked like.

I am sure God's creation of man is far different that what I just described. But in His grand design, He included the characteristic of free will. As people, we are free to choose what we do and believe. *"But if serving the LORD seems undesirable to you, then choose for yourselves this day whom you will serve."*[2].

Free will was in God's blueprint of man from the very beginning. Even Adam and Eve were given the freedom to do as they wanted in the Garden of Eden. In fact, the Bible speaks of choice many more times than the verse from Joshua above. Think about this; there would be no point in giving us the Ten Commandments if we weren't given the choice of whether or not to obey them. God could have simply programmed obedience into our DNA, and we would obey them automatically, kind of how we breathe automatically, or how we move our fingers from a hot stove automatically.

Here on earth we are free to do as we please. Take the freeway or city streets home? Mexican or Chinese tonight? We are free to honor God just as much as we are free to disobey Him. Have an affair? A not-so-ethical business deal? Pull the trigger? These are your decisions, and not Gods.

**The Fall of Man, or Original Sin**

Here's a summary of what happened:

God gave Adam the earth. The plants and the animals and all

## Why Does the World Suck so Bad?

the splendored sights, from the mountains to the oceans and all the breathtaking points in between—were all at Adams disposal. God gave Adam the Garden of Eden to care for, and in exchange allowed him to eat the fruit from any tree in the garden, except for one. *"Do not eat from the tree of knowledge of good and evil,"* said God, *"for if you do you will surely die."*[3]

God didn't tell Adam that if he ate from this tree, he would be banished to one of those tiny little islands with one coconut tree on it for two days. He didn't tell him he could only eat from the broccoli tree for a week if he got caught. No. God told Adam he would surely *die* if he ate from the tree of knowledge of good and evil.

In today's world, the death penalty is reserved for the most heinous of criminals. Murderers and rapists are the ones who face the consequence of death for their actions in modern society. God made it very clear that disobedience is not tolerated, and is punishable by death...and not the death where your heart stops beating. God was referring to an eternity apart from Him.

So, what happened? Adam ate from the tree. Actually, Eve gave Adam some fruit from the tree. Eve was deceived by a serpent, who told her that she wouldn't die by eating from the tree, but rather her eyes would be opened to the differences of good and evil, and she and Adam would then be like God.

What happened on that day created a rift between God and man that changed the course of humanity forever.

God cursed the ground. He made it produce thorns and thistles, and told Adam he would eat through "painful toil." "By *the sweat of your brow you will eat your food,"*[4] God said. Basically on that day, God created the concept of "work." If you've ever thought deeply about the concept of work and why we can't just play golf everyday, the fall of man may shed some light on the subject for you. My NIV study Bible defines toil as "burdensome labor." How relevant is that in terms of work in modern society? For me, it hits the nail on the head some days.

I'm not sure what His plans were before the fall; maybe we were to live in a utopian society where we would tend to weedless gardens, which would provide abundantly for us. Sure, we would have assignments to complete, but nothing too strenuous or stressful. It sort or reminds me of Santa's elves and the enthusiasm they have for making toys.

After the fall, that changed. God is telling us that He will still provide, but now we must *earn* our provisions. In the days of Adam and Eve, I imagine farming was one of the primary occupations. God mixed thorns and thistles—weeds—into the crops, just to make them more difficult to harvest.

Before the equipment we use today, cotton was hand-picked. Cotton plants have burrs on them; little thorns that will stick into your hands as you pick the cotton. The cotton pickers would endure much blood and pain, and eventually develop rough calluses on their fingers to withstand the torture of their work.

Today, we don't have much contact with thorns and thistles, but the symbolism is very relevant. Even with air conditioning, desk jobs, and much safer and humane working conditions, we still endure *mental* thorns at work each day: An overbearing

## Why Does the World Suck so Bad?

boss; an angry customer; an incorrect order, a calculation error. I remember my wife dreading going back to work the next day one Sunday night. "They don't call it fun, you know," she said. "They call it *work*."

CBS News aired a report recently which indicated only 45% of Americans were satisfied with their jobs. This means the majority of us don't like work...or at least the work God has given us to do. I guess his punishment still applies today.

I am not a professional author. Writing is merely an enjoyable hobby. My day job is employee benefit sales. If I were part of that CBS poll, I would probably include myself in that 45% of satisfied workers. But that doesn't mean I don't have my bad days. I think even those who truly love what they do experience some of the "painful toil" that God cursed man with through the original sin every once in a while. I can only imagine how different our society would be had we only obeyed.

God's curse of the ground was directed at Adam. To Eve He said, "*I will greatly increase your pains in childbearing.*"[5] What's unique about this verse, as well as man's painful toil, is God's grace in His judgment. Although now more painful, God is still granting woman the gift of having a child. As the owner of two kids, I can say that children may be God's single greatest gift to us. God could have pulled the plug on humanity with the original sin, but he didn't.

Ultimately, God banished Adam and Eve from the Garden of Eden. If you will recall, the Tree of Life was right next to the Tree of Knowledge of Good and Evil in the garden. With their eviction from the garden, they became separated from the Tree of Life. With this banishment, God was essentially separating man from Himself. The original sin was a sin. Sin separates man from God and His gift of eternal life. Humankind was off to a rocky start to say the least.

**Satan is Alive and Well**

Long before Adam and Eve, there was an angel who was *"the model of perfection, full of wisdom and perfect in beauty."*[6] The story continues that the angel was *"blameless in your ways until wickedness was found in you. Your heart became proud on account of your beauty, and you corrupted your wisdom because of your splendor. So I threw you to the earth..."*[7]

These few verses from Ezekiel 28 speak volumes about Satan. First, he was smart and handsome. Kind of reminds me of a movie star. People with looks and brains tend to be charismatic and highly influential. What happens next? It sounds like it went to his head; he became prideful. In fact, he felt that he was due the worship that only God is worthy. Because of this, God threw him to Earth.

Personally, it would have been fine with me if God threw him to Saturn, Jupiter, or maybe even a distant planet outside the solar system, but he was thrown to Earth instead. In some regards, this makes perfect sense. If Adam and Eve now know the difference between good and evil—it stands to reason that there must be evil in the world, so God gave us Satan. Once again, this was not God's doing as much as ours. God is only

## Why Does the World Suck so Bad?

providing what we asked for.

When Adam and Eve ate the forbidden fruit, it was a huge victory for Satan and his evil army. It proved that through free will, humans have the choice to obey or disobey God's word. This also proves that we are a vulnerable race, who can be easily deceived.

Satan is alive and well on this earth today. He is the fallen angel who opposes God and his plans. He promotes evil and corruption, and does so with the charm and charisma from his younger days. Satan's temptations come in many forms, most of which seem pleasurable at the time, but ultimately lead to destruction: A crooked business deal, an extra marital affair, an addiction. These are all things that feel pretty good when you first do them, but they will always ruin your life—or afterlife.

Since temptation comes in so many different forms, it's hard to see it coming. You see, Satan is running a covert operation here on earth. He's undercover. People are openly searching for God. You hear people crying out for Him, asking for His help in the most dyer of circumstances. But very few are openly crying out for Satan to come save them. Because of this, he can sneak around underground, and silently tempt us with worldly pleasures.

There's a show I watch on one of the cable networks called *American Greed.* It's a reality show about these crooked businessmen who get caught. Most of them are in jail; a few have committed suicide. Even our local paper has at least one good story each month about someone who got caught in a bogus business scheme. What baffles me about these people is how they think they are going to get away with their crimes. Obviously, the ones who do get away with it are not the ones in the paper or on TV — and there are probably thousands of them — but there are also lots and lots who end up in jail. I cannot help but think that these are the subtle temptations of Satan at work. He has a way of creating such a great desire for worldly things that people are willing to break the law — and risk losing everything — to obtain them.

This is just not for me. I want a beach house as bad as the next guy, but I'm not going to get one at God's expense. I would much rather sleep at night, and walk down the street without looking over my shoulder everyday. I guess I have a guilty conscious, but I could not bear the thought of having some federal official knocking on my door one day, ready to cuff me and take me away from my family for years and years. No way man.

So there you have it. The next time you hear of a robbery, a terrorist attack, a divorce, or any other crazy news, remember that there is a lethal combination of free will, sin nature and Satan-at-large on this earth. The mixture of these things makes this place pretty rough sometimes.

**We Are Free to Choose Jesus...or not**

A survey by ABC News and Beliefnet revealed that eighty-three percent of Americans are Christians. In other words, eighty-three percent have used their free will to *choose* Jesus as

## Why Does the World Suck so Bad?

their Lord and Savior. The remaining seventeen percent are agnostic, atheist, or a combination of non-Christian religions, such as Judaism, Muslim or Buddhism. The survey revealed that only thirty-three percent of the rest of the world are Christians; meaning sixty-seven percent of the earth's population is choosing not to accept Jesus as savior.

Doesn't this make sense? If we have the freedom to choose, then it stands to reason that not everyone is going to choose Christ. Otherwise, choice wouldn't be an option. Would we really want it any other way? I mean, a lawnmower has no choice. It turns on when I turn it on (or at least it's supposed to). A computer can only do what its programmer instructs it to do. What kind of life would we have if we had no choice in our actions? Sure, people choose to do evil things. But these evil acts only contrast with the good in the world. In a sense, good has no meaning without bad to offset it.

My wife bought our girls a kitten for Christmas a few years ago. (Our twelve year-old dog didn't have a clue that we were harboring a cat in our bathroom for three days without her knowledge.) When it came time to introduce the newest family member to the dog, it was a little chaotic. The kitten's fur stood straight up; she had her back arched and let out as ferocious of a hiss as she could muster. It sounded like a swipe of sandpaper on a board. The dog thought she was a furry snack of some kind; maybe like a peach with legs.

As they were facing off in our family room, both our girls wanted to scoop up the kitty and rescue her from pending death.

# WHY WORSHIP GOD?

But Kim and I motioned them back. "Leave them alone. Let them work this out on their own," I said. After a few more ferocious hisses, and some awkward circular dances by the dog, they finally accepted each other. They are best friends today.

If our dog tried to behead the cat, Kim and I would have most certainly stepped in. But we wanted to give them the freedom to greet each other their way, with no interference from us.

Do you think that's what God's attitude was toward Adam and Eve? He placed them in the garden, and even as Eve was being deceived by Satan, He exercised divine self-control to hold Himself back. "I've got to let them choose for themselves," He thought.

As I mentioned earlier, God made the consequences quite clear for our disobedience, and a sovereign God cannot go back on His own rules. In a way, this is comforting to me. If God says the wages of sin is death—and He is going to stick to it, then when Jesus says, "Whoever believes in Me has everlasting life," I can rest assured that is true as well. God is the one being in the universe who will never go back on His word.

**God is Always with Us**

Up to this point, I have made it sound like God has abandoned us; that we are all alone here. Nothing could be further from the truth! God is beside you right now. He is with you every step of the way, through the good and bad. Although He doesn't choose people's actions for them, He will stand beside you when other

# Why Does the World Suck so Bad?

people's actions cause tragedy in your life. He will be there to cry with you, and He alone can give you the strength to endure any chaos the world will throw at you.

The typical occupancy of the towers of the World Trade Center on any given business day was fifty-thousand people during business hours, not including visitors. On September 11, 2001—a Tuesday—there was less than half that number in the buildings at 8:46 am, when the first plane struck the north tower. 2,752 people died in the attacks on the World Trade Center. A horrific act of terrorism, which changed the landscape of the entire world; but the death toll was only a fraction of what it could have been. God could not stop the people responsible for this incredible act of violence, but He was certainly there, and He kept thousands away from those buildings on a day when they would have normally been there. Can you imagine how irritating it must have been to all the people stuck in traffic, had car trouble, or perhaps a sick child? Sometimes we can't see the blessings hidden in our roadblocks.

I decided long ago that the safest place to be in this dangerous and unpredictable world is close to God. I believe God will eagerly accept the invitation from anyone who sincerely asks him into his or her heart, so I want Him by my side. I talk to Him throughout the day, everyday. He is just as much a part of work as He is my home life. I want to study His word through the Bible and get to know Him. It is important to point out that inviting God into your life will not make you immune to this troubled world. Problems will come to the greatest Christian just as much as the coldest atheist. But, it is this relationship with

## WHY WORSHIP GOD?

God that will give you the strength and peace to endure the troubles that come your way, and this will make your stay on earth so much easier.

I have learned that God will make life's problems become much more manageable. God can help you through whatever obstacle you're facing by doing one very simple thing: *Ask!* "But God already knows my problems," you say to yourself. Sure He does, but He will not shower blessings upon your problems unless you humbly come to the throne and ask for His help. *"Ask and it will be given to you; seek and you shall find,"* Jesus tells us in Luke, chapter 9. *"For everyone who asks receives; he who seeks finds; and to him who knocks, the door will be opened."*[8] God will bless the sincere seeker. In Matthew 21, Jesus says, *"If you believe, you will receive whatever you ask for in prayer."*[9]

I find it funny that the fall of man occurs on page nine of my Bible—and the first seven pages are the introduction to Genesis and the creation of the heaven and earth! Really, we weren't around for even three pages before we messed things up. The rest of the Bible—all 1982 pages of mine—is about God trying to reconcile with man. The Bible is a book of love, written by a God of love. In the following chapters, we will explore all the mercy, grace and love that God extends to us, even in our most dyer moments. Celebrate, because we are loved by an Awesome God!

## Chapter Two:
# Change

**I**n the last chapter, I talked about how problems define our world. A day without them is much more the exception than the rule. I think another defining characteristic of this earth is change.

Everything is constantly changing. Just ten years ago, a music aficionado needed a large cabinet, wall, or even a room—to store his music collection. Today, you can hold it in the palm of your hand. What was once a bulky contraption tethered by a cord and

# WHY WORSHIP GOD?

used only for talking, a phone today is a multi-use mobile networking device, capable of texting, emailing, surfing the internet, taking pictures, and yes, even talking...it's completely wireless and works in your living room, a football stadium, or going seventy down the highway. I know we take that for granted these days, but it's still pretty amazing when you stop and think about it.

Change takes many forms outside of technology. It can be as insignificant as a stop light changing from red to green, or as big as someone whose perspective on life changes after an illness or tragedy. We change our clothes, our hairstyle, our paint color; even our baby's diapers. God gives us four seasons each year to keep things interesting. More so, the weather will even change on a daily—or hourly—basis. Don't like the weather? Stick around...it'll change. The landscape of our earth is constantly changing from both natural acts and man-made structures.

Think of your life of ten years ago compared to today. What has changed? I don't know you personally, but I would bet your life has seen incredible changes in ten years. Ten years ago, I was a single guy. Today I am married with two kids. I've lived in four different houses during that period and owned three different vehicles. Ten years ago, I had more hair and less belly than I have today.

There are only two things I can think of that don't change. One is God. God is anything but ever-changing. God is never-changing. He was exactly the same God a million years ago as he is today. He is exactly the same God today as he will be a million years from now. His word will never change. It's not like one day He'll say that the commandment about honoring your mother and father has become outdated and you don't have to obey it anymore. God will never put out a "Ten Commandments, Version 2.0."

I believe the contrast between a never-changing God and an ever-changing world is no mistake. It sends a daily message that we require much change during the course of our lives to one day become worthy of entering heaven. Only perfect people can enter heaven. If you're anything like me, you are probably far from perfect right now. But God is working on you. The Bible says, *"...he who began a good work in you will carry it on to completion until the day of Christ Jesus."*[1] This speaks to your evolution of one day becoming a perfect being, and all the changes you will endure to become that way. That's why the elderly always seem to be at peace more so than younger folks. They've lived more, learned more, and changed more; they are getting closer to perfection.

The other thing that doesn't change is the human spirit. Think about it. Our emotions are the same emotions we've always had, through all the generations. Happiness, sadness, envy, anger, and lust were every bit as prevalent in the humans from thousands of years ago as they are today. You think Cain was jealous of Abel because he had a better walking stick? Do you think they fought over it? It is quite possible. Cain was the hothead who murdered his brother after all. Regardless of the advancements in our world, the raw emotions humans feel do not change.

What this tells me is that, by eating the forbidden fruit, Adam and Eve permanently altered our human spirit. God instructed them not to eat from the Tree of Knowledge of Good and Evil. If they didn't know the difference between good and evil, this means that before eating the forbidden fruit, Adam and Eve were incapable of feeling negative emotions such as envy, greed, pride and lust. Can you imagine being incapable of feeling jealous about your neighbor's new car? Your neighbor pulls up in a new Lexus, and all you feel is pure, genuine happiness?

It wasn't until after committing the original sin that these bad emotions were woven into our character. Furthermore, the original sin represents the fall of mankind, and because of this, each one of us has inherited it. We are born fallen humans and possess the traits of jealousy, greed and all the other deadly sins. We didn't ask to be born with original sin…but you didn't ask for your skin and hair color either. They were given to you. Being born into sin is an inescapable trait of humanity, and you have no choice in the matter. And you can thank Adam and Eve for it.

Original sin separated man from God. Basically, Adam and Eve were telling God, "We don't need you. We can do this on our own."

**No Texting after Bedtime**

Our teenager has a cell phone. This is not unusual today. In fact, by Christmas break of her sixth grade year (yes, SIXTH grade), we thought she was either going to wake up dead, or perhaps get thrown out of school because she was—and I quote—"the only person in the entire school who didn't have a cellll phoooone..." (I had to drag it out for effect because that's kind of the way she was talking at the time.)

If you own one of these teenagers, you will probably agree that they are very unusual creatures. If I knew then what I know now, I would have picked a cell phone that didn't have the phone part...she wouldn't have known the difference. Really, they should just invent "texting machines" for teens, and leave the phone part off, because teens today do everything but talk to each other on the phone.

One of the rules associated with this device is that she is not to text after bedtime on school nights. Fair enough request in my book. After all, how is it possible to text after bedtime when you are sleeping? We made it very clear that the phone is a privilege, and not a right. Any violation of the rules would result in her losing her phone privileges for a period of time, depending on the violation.

For anyone out there with a cell phone, I'm sure you know your cellular phone company keeps some pretty good records regarding the usage of your device, and these can all be seen through your account on the carrier's website. (And if you are paying for a teenager's cell phone, then you absolutely have every right to monitor her usage without feeling like a snoop.) After reviewing Maddie's usage, it was with great shock to realize that our precious angel had been texting after bedtime! A blatant disregard for the rules!

Our carrier's website shows the time each text was sent, and it looks as if she was wrapping up a text conversation on the night in question. But the last text was after 9:10, so she definitely broke the rules.

As a parent, I struggle with fairness and harshness. Since it was her first offense, my initial reaction was to let her off with a warning. The only problem with this is that we had already set the ground rules. So, if we tell her one thing, then don't follow through with it, what kind of message does that send her? That rules don't really matter? Ultimately, Maddie lost her phone for two days. The rules were established, she broke them, and there were consequences. So be it.

Sure, Maddie messed up. No, it wasn't the end of the world. Yes, my wife and I were both mad. I mean, we gave her this nice thing out of the goodness of our hearts, and you would think she would have enough appreciation to honor the guidelines we established.

But you know what? It also hurt me that she broke the rules. When my child stumbles, I feel like maybe I failed in a way as well. I think disappointment affects the parent just as much as the punishment affects the child. In a way, it was a little heartbreaking to see her eyes as we took that phone from her. You could see the remorse; that she was sorry for what she did. But it was for her own good. In the end, punishing a child is more an act of love than anger.

How do you think God felt when Adam and Eve disobeyed him? My guess is that He was crushed. God gave them everything, and only asked for obedience in return. If we are

# Change

created in God's likeness and we have emotions, doesn't it stand to reason that God has emotions too? God made the rules; we broke them. God's word is absolute. He has to honor His own word. He has no choice. We separated ourselves from Him with our disobedience, and I bet that was a very difficult thing for Him.

The fall of mankind changed our world forever. It introduced evil to humankind and gave Satan a stronghold over humanity. Yes, a perfect God created the world, but through original sin it was us that made it imperfect.

Maddie breaks the rules and loses her cell phone. Tell me, is losing the phone my fault, or hers? If a person is caught speeding and gets a ticket, is the ticket the cop's fault, or the driver's? We should all be very aware that this world is the way it is, not because of God, but because of us.

# WHY WORSHIP GOD?

## Chapter Three:
## The Holy Spirit

In Chapter One, I talked about what a rough place the world can be, and how it was man's choice—not God's—that created this chaos. Despite our disobedience, God still loves us. He still wants us and has a purpose for us. Let's look at God's presence on Earth and how His love surrounds us, even in this fallen world.

Long ago, I heard a phrase which has stuck with me through the years: "We are kindest to the person we've never met." It might have been from a beer commercial, but I'm not sure. We are kindest to the person we've never met. Think about it. We hold the door for others. We'll let someone ahead of us at the grocery store check-out if they only have a jug of milk. If they have a bunch of groceries and spill them in the parking lot, we'll help them pick everything up. When we make eye contact with a stranger, it's usually accompanied with a smile, a nod and a soft "hello." If someone needs directions or the time, we are happy to oblige. For the most part, humans are pretty kind beings.

I'm a home improvement nerd. I'll try anything once. As my wife will testify, we've had some successes—and some failures—over the years. (We won't get into my plumbing skills and the numbers of floods I've caused.) I should also tell you that I drive a SUV. I am usually the guy leaving Home Depot with a load of stuff loaded so poorly, that even the slightest bump would send it crashing into the middle of the street. I am the guy you don't want to be behind in traffic if I'm carrying a load of construction materials. I'm easy to spot because I'm the one with the rear hatch open, with my load tied in with a shoestring or dental floss.

I remember trying to load some drywall into my vehicle once. Drywall has some unique characteristics. First, it's very heavy. It's flexible, too...but not too flexible. If you bend it too much it breaks. The drywall company also attaches two pieces together at the factory, I guess to irritate guys like me. This makes it twice as heavy. Since it's four feet wide, it has to go in the back of my vehicle at the perfect angle in order to fit, and even then about half the sheet hangs out of the back.

## The Holy Spirit

One day I was trying to wrestle two bound sheets of the stuff into my vehicle. It was so heavy and awkward to handle, I was having very little success loading it myself. That's when this nice gentleman offered to help. My first response was a polite, "No thank you," but when it was so obvious that I was attempting an impossible task, the guy insisted. In fact, he didn't insist; he just grabbed one end of it and started helping. You know, he didn't have to do that, especially after my kind brush-off, but he did. He helped for no reason at all.

Why is this? Why are we so kind to strangers? For the most part, we are much kinder to those we don't know compared to those we do know. I can sort of understand why. With a stranger, you have a clean slate. You don't know the person; therefore, you don't know that he hates your favorite team. You don't know that she has an annoying laugh, or that he got fired for stealing ten years ago. With a stranger, there are no preconceived prejudices to hold against the person. Besides, most everyone wants to make a good first impression.

That still doesn't explain our kindness, though. The only thing I can think of is that it is human nature. It is something born inside of us, and something that has existed since the beginning of humanity. Yes, there are some real jerks in the world, but this is the exception and not the rule. I mean, less than one percent of Americans are in jail. Most of us don't stand inside the elevator and watch the doors close as someone is running to catch it. We don't laugh at someone who tripped on the sidewalk and spilled her coffee all over the place (at least not to her face).

## WHY WORSHIP GOD?

Examples of love don't just come from adults either. I remember watching one of those home video shows, where a toddler—probably around two years old—gave his pacifier to a crying baby. It was a random display of kindness from someone way too young to know that's how you're *supposed* to act.

A co-worker told me her third-grade son was denied lunch the other day because his "lunch account" was out of money. She was perturbed that the school failed to notify her that his account was running low, but it was more disturbing that the lunchroom personnel let him walk his tray down the food line and pick all his food. It wasn't until he got to the register that they snatched his lunch tray from him and replaced it with a pack of crackers. You know what his classmates did? These eight year-old children shared their lunch with him. He got chicken nuggets from one kid, half a roll from another, a sugar cookie and pudding. How cool was that? People will help people out of rough spots, regardless of age.

So, where does this innate kindness come from? What tells us the difference between right and wrong? That we shouldn't lie or steal? Or that unkind words will hurt someone's feelings? One reason we know this is because the Bible gives us some rules to follow. The Ten Commandments are the most distinct, but there are hundreds of other handy tips in the Bible that tell us how we ought to live our lives and treat others.

Furthermore, the Bible tells us that there are consequences. Ecclesiastes 12:14 says, *"For God will bring every deed into judgment,*

## The Holy Spirit

*including every hidden thing, whether it is good or evil."* Jesus talks about facing judgment often in the New Testament as well. This tells us that we are going to have to answer for every crappy thing we did while on this earth. For many believers, it makes us think twice about our actions. Kind of a discipline by fear technique.

So, yes, kindness can be learned, but it seems to be more instinctive than trained. After all, when you see someone in need, you don't pull out your Bible to check and see if you supposed to help or not. Besides, there are a lot of people out there that couldn't tell the difference between a Bible and a cookbook. Kindness happens without hesitation. There is a force in the universe that drives our morals and behaviors toward good, more so than bad.

As much as we are born with original sin, we are also born with the Holy Spirit. There is this little piece of God in each of us that involuntarily responds to others with love. There is no other way to explain it. It is something we are born with, and it dwells inside each one of us.

A good friend of mine lives on the Mississippi Gulf Coast. When hurricane warnings were posted back in 2005 for Katrina, he made the decision to ride out the storm at a local shelter. My buddy almost died in that storm, not because of Katrina, but because he convinced his wife not to evacuate. She almost killed him.

Luckily, Scott and his wife survived the storm unharmed, with very little damage to their home and business. Once he was able to get his stuff back in order, Scott literally drove around looking for ways to help. He helped remove fallen trees from roadways and houses, he helped clear debris off people's property so they could re-enter their homes. He helped to repair damaged buildings to make them safe enough to enter. Scott played the Good Samaritan for several weeks after the storm.

Having known Scott for a long time, I can say that church never really was his thing. Don't get me wrong—this doesn't make him a bad guy. On the contrary, he is a great guy with a huge heart. I'm just illustrating the point that despite not being a big church guy, Scott was still driven to help so many after Katrina. Nobody told him to go clear roadways; he certainly didn't read it in a Bible. There is just something in his soul that makes him want to help others. That something is the Holy Spirit. It dwells in every one of us...like our own little piece of Jesus.

The Holy Spirit is the unseen force that keeps this insane world sane enough to function. Yes, there are crazy people and criminals and terrorists, but they make up a tiny fraction of humanity. Remember, there is free choice and evil among us. It's part of this world. But even with the insanity, the vast, vast majority of people have this natural love in their hearts. And we can thank God for it.

Chapter Four:

# A World without God

**I** am German, but I've never been to Germany. I understand there is a system of highways in Germany that don't have speed limits, called the Autobahn. To me, the concept of no speed limit is pretty cool. My mother lives about two-hundred miles from me. The drive is normally three and a half hours, but if I could drive one-hundred miles an hour, it would only take two hours. If I could drive two-hundred miles per hour, I could get there in just

# WHY WORSHIP GOD?

an hour. Granted, I drive a seven year-old truck that will barely go eighty, but that is merely a detail. If I were allowed to drive two-hundred miles per hour, I would certainly find a way to do so.

I live in a suburb outside of Memphis, called Germantown. Germantown is a quiet little residential community, which in my opinion is a very nice place to live. Our children can stomp the neighborhood without too much worry. We know all of our neighbors, and we are all very cordial to each other (for the most part). Our neighborhood is pretty stable, too; most of the families have lived here for years, and no one really wants to move.

If you ever find yourself in Germantown, Tennessee, may I offer you a word of advice? Don't speed. In fact, don't even think about speeding, because the police have ESP radar that can tell them when you are even *thinking* about speeding. I think Germantown is the only city in America where you can go straight to jail for speeding. No trial necessary; just straight to jail. I haven't seen one of my neighbors in months. I'm starting to think it's because he was going forty on Farmington Road. (The speed limit is thirty-five.)

I'm embarrassed to admit it, but I appreciate the strict law enforcement in my town. I was like most teenage boys with an innate desire to drive as fast as humanly possible, and even today, I like the thought of driving 200 miles an hour on a rural German highway. But in local traffic, these fast drivers tend to stress me out. I guess I'm getting old, but having everyone crawling down the street at the same speed as me is a relaxing

# A World Without God

thing. Keeping crazy drivers under control only makes this town a more desirable place for me to live.

What if there were no speed limits—not on the open highway—but right in the middle of your town? What if there were no stop signs, either? Better yet, what if there were speed limits and stop signs, but no law enforcement? Can you imagine the chaos? There would be wrecks at every turn. In theory, you could get to your destination much faster if there weren't speed limits and stop signs slowing you down. In reality, it would probably take five times as long because of all the wrecks in your way.

So, let's take this one step further and just imagine life without any laws whatsoever; a free-for-all. There is no doubt that evil would be even more prevalent than it is today. Murders and burglaries would be the mainstay of society. Why not? There would be no consequences for your actions. We've all heard of people who sleep with shotguns by their beds. Well, in a society without laws it would be mandatory.

In the last chapter, I talked about how God's holy presence regulates our behavior; how we are born with a "love instinct" for the most part, and kindness comes naturally. We learn that we will stand before God in judgment one day for our lives on earth. Knowing that there are consequences for how we live our earthly lives may very well dictate how we act. I mention this because I believe a society without laws would be crazy and dangerous indeed, but kindness and love through the Holy Spirit would still exist. If there wasn't a law against theft, our conscious

## WHY WORSHIP GOD?

would still tell most of us that it is wrong to steal. But, how many of us would follow God's law even if there were no earthly laws? I think the temptation would be too great for us weak humans to handle. Even with God's presence, I think you'd agree that our society could not function without rules for us to follow.

So, the next time you are parked on the side of the road with those bright blue strobes in your rear-view mirror—and more than likely at least one person you know passing by—try to remember that our society wouldn't exist without laws and the enforcement of them. Our laws are what allow us to walk freely down the street.

Can you imagine what the world would be like if there were no God? The world without heaven? A world where this is it. When you're gone, you're gone. There are no sins to answer for because there is no such thing as eternal life. When you really think about it, a world without God is a world without love...would we even have emotions at all?

Would you behave any differently if there were no God?

I'll tell you how I would be. I would be in it one-hundred percent for myself. You have to remember that the Holy Spirit that dwells within me—and fills me with love and kindness toward others—would no longer exist. I would be the dirtiest businessman you can imagine. I would lie to your face over and over again just to make a buck. I would probably cheat on my wife—many times—if there was even such a thing as marriage. I would cut in line at the grocery store, and if a stranger needed help...forget it. My goal would be to have beach houses, mountain houses, yachts, trips, really cool watches. I would want to live the most lavish lifestyle I could. I really wouldn't stop at anything to achieve it. You only get one shot...might as well make it count. Whoever dies with the most toys definitely wins.

I don't think I'd be alone in my actions either. I bet most people would have the same mentality as me.

A world without God would be different in more ways than we can fathom. There would be no eternal life, no divine goal to work toward. For many of us, the only thing that gets us through life's tragedies is the promise of entering heaven, where our earthly struggles don't exist. When we lose a loved one, we hold onto the hope of being reunited with that person for eternity. In a world without God, that hope would not exist. For most, our will to live would be greatly reduced, even eliminated, without God.

Second, the Holy Spirit—the invisible force of goodness that is the pulse of the earth—would not exist. The spirit of kindness woven into the fabric of humanity would be replaced by a spirit of selfishness and indulgence. The sick neighbor would have to deal with her sickness alone, without a hot meal or help with her kids.

Prayer is therapy to me. Philippians chapter 4 says, *"Do not be anxious about anything, but in everything, by prayer and petition, with thanksgiving, present your requests to God."* (Here is the best part.) *"And the peace of God, which transcends all understanding, will guard your hearts and minds in Jesus Christ."*[1] I cannot testify how true that last sentence is for me. There is nothing a prayer doesn't help. Whether it is a problem with Kim or the kids, or if someone close to me is going through medical, financial, or some other type crisis. If I've gotten myself in a jam at work I don't know how to get out of...I have learned, albeit slowly, to pray about it. There is not a request too small for God to listen to. I can literally tell Him everything. As anyone who prays knows, sometimes God says yes, sometimes no, and sometimes you just have to wait. But aside from the end result of the prayer is the peace. A prayer calms the soul, and even long before God answers, you receive the calming side-effect of your prayer, which is peace. I can't tell you how much a prayer settles an anxious heart.

If there were no God, prayer wouldn't exist. So, not only would we not have the luxury of communicating with the one who can actually solve our problems, we wouldn't enjoy the calming side-effect of peace, either.

**The Big House**

I have a friend—who has a friend—who was recently released from prison. I won't bore you with the details, but this guy served four months for a bogus business deal. He didn't serve in the maximum-security tank you see in the movies; he was in a minimum security facility, or "white collar prison," as some people call it.

This place didn't have a concierge or tee-times available. There wasn't room service or a masseuse on staff. But, according to my friend, it was still somewhat cushy. First, there wasn't a fence, nor did the cell doors lock. They had television, internet, telephones, and every morning there was a copy of USA Today and the Wall Street Journal at their disposal. They could watch movies in the common areas, do crafts, read and even cook. Only problem was, you couldn't leave. That place had just about everything but freedom, and freedom is precious. Sure, the door was wide open and there was no gate to jump over. But that doesn't mean there aren't prison guards watching. Most of the inmates are educated, and almost no one is incarcerated longer than five years. These prisoners are smart enough to know that their stay is temporary, and the wisest thing they can do is just serve their time without causing problems or trying to escape.

The most interesting thing about the story was how these "white collar" prisoners checked-in. They begin their sentence at the maximum security prison not far away, where they are strip-searched, given their prison garb and other provisions. This is the cold, hard, mortar-colored compound you see in the movies. My friend's friend had to spend several hours in a holding cell—complete with a concrete floor, steel doors, and a toilet in the corner—with convicted murderers and rapists in adjacent cells. This was his first impression of prison; at the time, he thought medium-security was going to be just as bad. He thought he was in for hard time, and probably wondered if he would even survive.

The stories from the "Big House" were incredible. They only serve boneless chicken because the inmates will turn the bones into knives. The plastic reinforcements on the corners of the banana crates are removed before they're brought in because they can be turned into weapons as well. There is actually hierarchy

## WHY WORSHIP GOD?

among the inmates, and new prisoners must honor this "self-government," or face consequences. Drug use runs rampant, the violence is ever-present, and there are more attempted escapes than the media would ever reveal. If you are serving thirty years to life for a heinous act with no chance of parole, then the hope of returning to society to rebuild your life is all but gone.

There is a stark contrast between the culture in the medium-security versus the maximum-security prison. The reason for the difference boils down to one word: Hope. In the white-collar lock-up, the inmates know their stay is only temporary. They understand that they will be given the chance to reunite with their families and try to piece their lives back together one day. In the big house, that hope doesn't exist. The "lifers" know that they will die within those cinder block walls, or at least spend the prime years of their lives there. They know their stay is permanent, and that good behavior doesn't mean a thing. Since there is no hope, they don't really care about their actions. They can be barbarians.

To me, my friend's prison story illustrates what earth would be like if there were no God. God means hope, and hope is a powerful word. Hope tells us that there is something better; that this world is not our home. Our home is in heaven with Jesus. For many, the hope of eternity with God is the only thing that gets them out of bed each day. I think people in a world without God would probably act a lot like those life-timers in the big house. It would be a world without hope.

Have you ever noticed how whenever something bad

# A World Without God

happens, something good usually follows? My wife has bursitis. She is in a walking boot and enduring much discomfort. She has a hard time working, and even doing chores around the house. Because of this, other families have stepped up to help her with carpool duties for Maddie's cheerleading practice, and we've even had meals delivered to our house.

When my failed business venture was putting me closer and closer to foreclosure a few years ago, friends and relatives stepped up and lent me the money I needed to survive. We have just about closed that chapter in our lives, thanks to their kindness.

When a nine year-old girl in our community fought cancer, and the medical bills became overwhelming, dozen of friends, schools and church groups conducted fundraisers to raise thousands of dollars for her cause.

More times than not, good counteracts bad. The sad part is that the bad is usually so overwhelming that we can't see the good things that come out of it. For that sick girl in our community, nobody tapped elbows and whispered to each other how awesome it was to raise all that money. The focus was on the tragedy of the illness, not of the goodness of those who were touched by it. Can you think of a storm in your life, and the good that came out if it?

So, which world would you prefer—a world without God, or a world with Him? Would anyone want to live in a world without love, kindness, and the power of prayer? Would anyone want to live in a world in which there was no future hope? Would you really live a fulfilling life knowing that once you were gone, you were gone? To me, these are silly questions. If you think the world is a bad place now, just imagine how bad it would be if there were no God. It would uninhabitable. Sure, I'll take a German highway with no speed limits, but when it comes to my life, I would accept nothing other than having God's loving spirit watching over us all. That's really the only way the world can function.

We take the good things in this world for granted. We expect goodness, and it is the benchmark in which we compare all other behavior. I don't think we realize that kindness in the world is purely a gift from God to us. Remember, He didn't have to give us this, but through mercy and grace His loving spirit covers the entire planet, and all the good things on earth come from Him. And we can thank God for it.

Chapter Five:
# The Hope Exchange

**I** want a Nissan 370Z, black. It doesn't have to be new; it doesn't even have to be this year's model. It needs to have low miles, with leather interior and a sunroof. I want a sunroof, not to open it, but just for the light to come in. I don't like open sunroofs. It feels like the wind is pulling out what's left of my hair. Also, it can't be my primary car. It has to be an extra car. You see, a Nissan 370Z only has two seats. How can I haul around the family with two seats? Besides, I don't want to put all those miles on such a choice automobile.

I really want a Porsche Cayman, however I like to keep my fantasies realistic.

So, what do I do? I wake up everyday and go to work. Maybe working toward that dream. Until then, I'm stuck with the family truckster. I have to admit, a 370Z is sort of happy place for me. If I've had a rough day, I can close my eyes at night and dream about what it would like to have that car. The speed, the handling, the looks. I know; my dreams are kind of pathetic.

My wife and I are in a constant debate over a lake house versus a beach house. The lake house is only an hour away, but it's by a lake. The beach house is by the beach, but that's eight hours away. Really, all that's in store for us right now is our house house. I guess we should be happy with what we're given, but it never hurts to dream.

When our youngest daughter Emma was three, she decided she wanted a Dora the Explorer castle for Christmas. "I want a Dowa casuhl fow Kwismus," she would say. Over and over again, all she talked about was that toy. I wonder if she dreamed her little toddler self to sleep every night in her big-girl bed, thinking about how cool she would be if she had that Dora castle. I wonder if she thought she would actually *become* Dora if she had it. Maybe she thought she would be the most popular toddler on the block if she only had her casuhl.

We told her if she wanted the Dora castle, then she was going to have to ask Santa for it when we went and saw him at the mall.

# The Hope Exchange

This is the confusing part. That year, all Emma did was scream when she saw Santa. We barely got her to stay on his lap long enough for the overpriced photo. We're still not sure how Santa learned of her wish, but nonetheless, on Christmas morning he delivered the Dora castle she most desperately wanted.

We didn't make it to New Years before that toy was forgotten. I don't think the garbage truck had come to remove the box it came in—along with all the other packing and wrapping materials from Christmas morning—before she forgot about it.

Last spring, Emma saw that toy in the yard sale pile and freaked out. "I like my Dora castle," she said. "I've been looking for it for a long time. Can we *not* sell it?" First off, you're almost six. Second, that thing has been in the attic for two years and you haven't mentioned it. No, we are not going to *not* sell it.

Truth is, the anticipation far outweighed the receiving of the Dora castle. Emma had more fun *hoping* for that toy than she actually had playing with it. Aren't we all guilty of that sometimes? We get the idea that something—a gadget, an outfit, a car, a new relationship, a new job—is going to change our lives and bring us a level of happiness we've never experienced before. So we pine for it. We dream about it. We save for it. We might even buy it with the credit card.

Sometimes, it works. You find the relationship that becomes a marriage. You keep a car until it's actually paid off. You stay at a job long enough to have to re-order business cards. But most of the time, when we finally get the thing we've been hoping for, it ends up not nearly as great as we thought it would be. It ends up in the yard sale pile. Like Emma's Dora Castle, the hoping part was way more fun than the thing itself.

That is the beauty of hope. It keeps us going.

The Bible makes an interesting observation about hope:

*"For in this hope we were saved. But hope that is seen is no hope at all. Who hopes for what he already has? But if we hope for what we do not yet have, we wait for it patiently."* [1]

What this verse tells me is that once you receive what you've been hoping for, the hope goes away. I call it the Hope Exchange. Once Emma received the Dora Castle, she could no longer hope for it. It was a trade-off; the hope for the object.

Our first house had some unfinished attic space over the garage, which I so boldly volunteered to finish out one year. We decided to make it our playroom. We completed our sketches and materials list in October, and our goal was to have the room ready for Maddie's birthday in late January. We thought a slumber party would be a great way to christen our new playroom. Although I had never taken on a task of this size, I felt that three months would surely be enough time to have it ready. Famous last words. That room was finished in May of the following year. What we thought would take three months took seven.

## The Hope Exchange

I spent just about every spare moment up in that room, running my wire, ductwork, and hanging the insulation and drywall. I did the majority of the work myself, and I must admit, it was a big job. BIG job. I don't think I'll ever do a project like that again. After about the third or fourth month, I grew weary, yet I kept plugging along. I started to dread the thought of having to go up there and work after working my real job everyday—as opposed to sinking into the couch with a remote.

Do you know what kept me going? The thought of the finished project. My vision of us hanging out in that nice room, with smooth, painted walls (they weren't that smooth in some places), working outlets, new carpet and furniture. As tired as I was of working in that cold, dusty attic, I knew one day it would pay off. I was working toward a goal, and really, a goal is simply hope with a deadline. If I started working on a bonus room that would never get finished, would I even bother to start?

If you knew that you would never get to retire, would that change how you feel about work? Most of us try to work hard with the hope of retiring one day. If I knew I could never retire—regardless of my job performance or how much money I saved—I would probably not care about my work nearly as much as I do. But that's not the case. One day I WILL get to retire, and because of this, I work hard today. I try to earn more—to save more—to maybe retire earlier than planned. Do you see how valuable the principal of hope is? It is hope that drives me to work hard every day. Hope puts the end in mind; it is the fuel of the human spirit.

If you understand the principal of the hope exchange, why on

## WHY WORSHIP GOD?

earth would anyone want to win millions in the lottery? On the surface, that sounds like a crazy statement. Of course anybody would want to be a millionaire. But, stop and think about it for a minute. Why would anyone want to trade all their dreams for cash? You see, I have goals...the beach house, my sports car, my retirement. These are the things that motivate me to go out and do something productive each day. If, all of the sudden, all these things were handed to me, what would I have to look forward to in life? What would happen to my motivation to be productive? I would have exchanged all of my hope at once in the form of a winning lottery ticket. I would instantly have my sports car, my beach house, and my retirement. These things wouldn't have nearly the value as if I had worked hard and earned them. Once you've got it all, what is left to hope for? I would get bored easily with my possessions, and search for fulfillment elsewhere, which could be destructive. I think that's why we hear stories of how the lottery ruins people's lives. It takes their hope away.

Hope is the gift from God that gets us through the day, the week, even the year. On my way to another long day of work, I can think about the vacation next month, and it seems to put my job back in perspective. You can hope for a great concert that you are planning to see. You can hope for a fun cookout with friends, or that the holidays this year will be the best ever. If there is a bad season in life, the future is almost always looked upon with optimism. That is called hope. It keeps us plugging along.

We also use hope to describe some serious circumstances in life. "I hope the biopsy comes back negative," you say. "Oh, I hope the rumors aren't true," you think. "I really hope I'm not

## The Hope Exchange

affected by the lay-off," you pray. In all its contexts, hope is a term that describes positive anticipation of a future event...in other words, wishful thinking. Hope is like a carrot-on-a-stick in a sense.

Sometimes, we will gladly exchange our hope for an outcome. You will be just fine trading the *hope* of a negative biopsy for an *actual* negative biopsy. You're glad to know that the lay-offs have been settled and you weren't affected. But sometimes this doesn't happen. Sometimes the thing you hoped for doesn't end up the way you wanted. And this leads to a whole new hope. It just keeps going.

Other times, hope runs out. "Our dog ran away over a month ago, and we're starting to lose hope." "The doctor said there is very little hope left for Grandma." It is during these times that we lean on the spiritual hope that comes from God.

In biblical terms, hope becomes even more powerful than our earthly definition. The biblical definition of hope is "confident expectation."

I promised Kim a trip to Hawaii for our fifth wedding anniversary. On our fifth wedding anniversary, she got a card and a promise to take her to Hawaii on our *tenth* anniversary. I can dream about that trip, and hope that we are able to go when our ten-year milestone finally arrives. But, the day that the Hawaiian hotel is reserved and the flight is booked, our dream trip becomes more than just a dream. When the book on "What to Do in Hawaii" appears, when oatmeal pies get replaced with vegetables in our kitchen, and when clothing store bags start multiplying in Kim's closet, we will then have the *confident expectation* that we are going to Hawaii. We still hope for it, but this hope changes. It turns from an "if we go" to a "When is it going to get here?" kind of hope. It turns from a dream to anticipation.

Jesus Christ died on the cross so you and I can be joined with Him for eternity. If we place our hope in Jesus, then His word says we will go to heaven. Nobody has ever seen someone actually enter heaven's gates. But, since we trust God's word as absolute, we live with the *confident expectation* that we will enter heaven by accepting Jesus as our Lord and Savior. This is not something that may or may not happen, like our earthly hope. Even though we've never actually seen it, our faith gives us the confidence to believe it's true. *"For I know the plans I have for you," declares the Lord, "plans to prosper you and not to harm you, plans to give you hope and a future."*[2]

Maybe one day when my kids are educated, married and off the payroll for good, I may actually get that little black sports car. Kim and I may one day end the debate of the beach house vs. the lake house...or maybe just get a condo in the mountains. When we do, we will have exchanged our dream for the real thing.

But the exchange that really matters is the hope of eternity with Jesus for an eternity with Jesus. And Jesus tells us that exchange is guaranteed. That sports car and vacation home won't mean much in a hundred years, but God's promise of eternity in heaven, that is the Hope Exchange that trumps all others. In this regard, it really doesn't matter whether I ever get a

370Z. God gives me the only hope that really matters, and I thank Him for it.

# WHY WORSHIP GOD?

Chapter Six:
# God's Gifts for Us All

**I**t's a fact. Some people live in mansions while others live in apartments. Some people get iPhones while I get…well, I really don't know what mine is called. But it's not as cool as an iPhone, that's for sure. Some people do better with the opposite sex, some people are better at sports, and some people have a knack for making money. Let's accept it. We are all different, and God has blessed us all with different gifts. Now, before we get sidetracked into

# WHY WORSHIP GOD?

a discussion about how it's unfair that you can't play the guitar or your lawnmower isn't self-propelled like your neighbors, let's take a moment to look at ways in which God has blessed us all.

I love to watch those animal shows, especially the violent ones that show the animals eating each other. It is fascinating. And hey, before you get all grossed-out about animals eating each other, just remember that we do the same thing. Our animals just have grill marks on them. The narrator of these shows is always some Australian or British fellow. He talks quietly, as if he's there or something…like the animals are going to hear him and attack.

I remember watching this show about the wildebeests in Africa. You know, they look kind of like deer. The wildebeests were all standing in the shallow water, getting some relief from the brutal African heat. The Australian narrator was talking about their drinking habits oh so softly, when all of the sudden….SNAP! CRUNCH! An African croc comes out of nowhere, and a muddy, bloody scene ensues. The croc nabs his prey through the splashing water and fleeting herd. They always show the scene in slow motion, as each splash creeps horizontally across the screen, while the Australian guy rambles on. The wildebeests finally make it to dry land, and run as fast as their skinny legs will allow…except one. Poor fellow. What a tragedy. That wildebeest was probably a husband, a father…a friend. And in the blink of an eye, he becomes dinner.

What struck me as weird is that fifteen minutes after that

## God's Gifts for us All

horrific scene, the wildebeests return to the same exact place in the shallow water, and the process starts all over again. Generation upon generation of wildebeests have been eaten by generation upon generation of crocs, and they haven't figured out a safer way to get a drink? After thousands of years, fish still think that worms miraculously float in the middle of water? Mice haven't learned that the thing with cheese in it isn't a serving platter?

The one thing God has given man, which He did not give the animals, is the ability to communicate at a high level. Sure, I know my cat is hungry when she stares at me and meows, but she hardly has the ability to talk about her day. I read an article that estimated the number of different species of animals to be somewhere between three and thirty million. We only know about two million of them. Millions of different animals on the planet; not one with communication skills anywhere close to that of humans.

Archeologists have found primitive writing and drawings dating back thousands of years. Around 3,000 B.C., the first words were chiseled on some clay tablets. This was the dawn of recordkeeping; man's ability to record events and memories for others to see long after the author is gone. It was arguably the most significant technological advancement in the history of mankind. The tablets were eventually replaced by papyrus paper, then the printing press, the typewriter, the computer...you get the chronology.

So, not only do we communicate at a superior level compared

to our animal friends, we can actually learn from prior generations through recorded events. We can stand on the shoulders of the last generation and capitalize on their discoveries. If only the wildebeests knew about this!

**We All Have Gifts**

God has given each one of us individual gifts. Romans 12 says, *"We have different gifts, according to the grace given us. If a man's gift is prophesying, let him use it in proportion to his faith. If it is serving, let him serve; if it is teaching, let him teach; if it is encouraging, let him encourage; if it is contributing to the needs of others, let him give generously; if it is leadership, let him govern diligently; if it is showing mercy, let him do it cheerfully."*[1]

Do you know someone who says they don't have any talents? Any "gifts?" Either they haven't discovered their talent yet, or maybe their talent is whining. God has given each of us things that we can do better than others. I can't sing; I've played guitar for years, but I'm no good. My golf score requires a calculator most days. But I enjoy writing, and I am an above average woodworker. I know a guy who is an incredible guitarist, but he couldn't nail two boards together if he took a course. There are great athletes, great chefs, great parents, great businessmen and women, but nobody can be great at everything. We just weren't made that way. I think God smiles when we find our talents and use them to the fullest. I think He smiles even more when we use our gifts to glorify Him.

God made Alexander Graham Bell and Thomas Edison good

inventors. They used their gifts to create two significant inventions, the phone and the light bulb. After Bell and Edison, two more gifted inventors came along and improved the phone and light bulb. After that, two more came along and did the same thing. Generation after generation are using their God given gifts to create or improve something. Do you see how God has a hand in the evolution of our society?

All these advancements have merely been improvements on the idea that came to life when man first chiseled on that clay some five-thousand years ago. I wonder what those first words were (maybe that there were crocs in the water). The cumulative result of five-thousand years of development encapsulates the world today. In essence, that cool cell phone next to you is the result of five millenniums of research. Almost everyone in this country gets to enjoy the advancements in communication through cell phones and the internet, and almost everyone gets to enjoy television and music. These are gifts from God that we can all enjoy, regardless of our income or social class.

There is no doubt these are magical times in terms of electronics. But medicine, architecture, entertainment, and transportation are also highly advanced, thanks to the pioneering efforts of our ancestors. As Americans, we are blessed to have access to the finest healthcare in the world. I understand there is a dear monetary price associated with this, but the quality of care in this country is keeping us around longer and longer.

And we can thank God for it. Remember, He didn't have to do it this way. He could have stopped our progress at the caveman level. What if we never learned to write? We could just as easily still be in caves, wearing buffalo skins and communicating through grunts and burps. I don't know about you, but I kind of like electricity and central heat!

## Community

The result of this evolution is the civilization we have today, and our need for each other lets us share in each other's discoveries. It's called community. Each person's contributions to our progress get to be enjoyed by all. Again in Romans 12, we read, *"Just as each of us has one body with many members, and these members do not all have the same function, so in Christ we who are many form one body, and each member belongs to all the others. We have different gifts, according to the grace given us."*[2] God didn't make us to be secluded from each other; He made us to interact with one another. Alexander Graham Bell didn't invent the telephone just to keep for himself.

Because of this, we have great medicine because of the gifts of doctors and scientists; we have technology thanks to the electronics and software developers. The architects have given us stronger homes; the philosophers and professors give us knowledge; the farmers give us food; the preachers give us religion. The list goes on and on. Each person's individual contributions are thrown into the melting pot of society.

Did you know that orangutans are solitary creatures? Males and females come together just a few days for mating, and mothers will stay with their cubs for about five years. Other than that, they spend their lives alone. God could have made us solitary beings. But with our intelligence and emotions, it would be an awful existence to spend life alone. One of the worst punishments a prisoner receives is solitary confinement. The reason is because man was not meant to be alone. We are social creatures. In Genesis, God spoke, *"It is not good for man to be alone."*[3] We all know that the greatest stories of our lives are about people, not objects. On our death bed, we want to be surrounded by loved ones and not our jewelry collection.

**A Government Created by God**

One of God's promises is to meet our needs. Philippians 4 says, *"And my God will meet all your needs according to his glorious riches in Christ Jesus."*[4] We are fortunate to live in a country where these basic needs are met. In America (and other industrialized nations), everyone is provided food, shelter, and clothing. We are offered a free education, and we can get a college degree in this country if we are willing to work for it.

There are laws in place designed to protect us, and we have police that enforce these laws. We have the armed forces, which protect our country from outside threats. We have civil servants who come to our aid in the event of a medical emergency, fire, or natural disaster. If we are accused of wrongdoing, we are given the right to a fair trial.

For many, these basic needs are provided by the government. I understand that leading a nation like the United States lends itself to much scrutiny and late-night TV jokes. But you cannot argue with the fact that our government provides and protects. Does all this work perfectly? Of course not. How can anything be perfect in an imperfect world?

So, how does our government find its way into a book about God? Because the establishment of authority was created by God. Romans, Chapter 13 says *"Everyone must submit himself to the governing authorities, for there is no authority except that which God has established. The authorities that exist have been established by God."*[5]

Our founding fathers relied on God's direction in their decision to break away from England and start their own country. There are four references to God in the Declaration of Independence. "In God We Trust" is one of America's most recognized slogans, and it can be found on every single piece of U.S. currency. A sad irony is that our forefathers relied heavily on God's guidance when establishing our country, yet, today's society is trying to push Him out of it. That breaks my heart, but probably not nearly as much as it breaks His.

**A Savior for Everyone**

We can talk about God's earthly gifts all day. We can talk about this beautiful planet He gave us to explore, the way that He provides at just the right moment, or the wisdom and peace that He can deliver if we would only ask. But, the most important gift God offers to us all is the gift of salvation. This was done through Jesus. When Jesus died on the cross, He took on the sins of the world. This is because man is not worthy to save himself;

he can't do it through his own deeds. All our daily struggles seem to fade in this divine picture of an eternity in a perfect heaven with a perfect God.

I think about my life today. I get to come home to an air-conditioned house and eat a hot meal prepared on my electric stove. I can then go outside and play with the kids until dark, then read by a lamp, watch TV, browse the web or even write this book. I can take a warm shower to end my day and fall asleep in a soft bed. On the weekends, we can go to the zoo, or to the movies, and go out to eat at a good restaurant. To some, my life sounds a little dull; to others, it might sound kind of nice. Regardless, most of us get to enjoy the same things I do in some fashion.

I've always felt that this kind of life was created more by man than by God. I was wrong. It is through God's love for us and His mercy that we enjoy the civilization we have today. Our modern society exists today because God allows it to. So, when you finish your next home-cooked meal, and sit down to watch TV or read, thank God for it.

## Chapter Seven:
# The Gift of Earth

The year was 1976. The car was a 1976 Buick Regal, blue two-door. I was eight years old. My parents, brother and I traveled that year to Phoenix and back. We took pit stops in Dallas to go to Six Flags, Grand Canyon National Park, and then to Phoenix to stay with my aunt and uncle. They owned a vacation home in Mexico, so we went there for a few days before returning to Phoenix and finally back home to Little Rock.

# WHY WORSHIP GOD?

As an eight year-old, I didn't really have a clue as to how long I was in the car or how far it was. Furthermore, in 1976, there were no iPods, cell phones, portable DVD players or hand held video games. If I remember correctly, I think I took an old cigar box and filled it with stuff to do, and I can only imagine how many hours I spent fighting with my brother (and moving my hand over the imaginary line dividing the back seat). But honestly, I must have been bored out of my skull. With the help of technology, I went back recently and calculated the distance and windshield time of that trip; 3,400 miles and fifty-one hours and eighteen minutes. More than an entire work week in the back seat of that car without a seat belt.

If there is a plus to my technology-deficient childhood, it has to be that I spent much of my time on that trip looking out the window. After all, isn't that why my parents took us on that grueling journey in the first place? To allow us to see this beautiful country of ours? Having spent the majority of my life in Arkansas at that point, I had never seen a cactus, ocean, or a hole the size of the Grand Canyon. When I look back on that trip, even today it stands out as one of the great adventures of my childhood. I got to explore a piece of this great land of ours.

In a family of eight, trips to places like Disney World were outside the realm of financial reality. For us, summer vacation meant visiting relatives, usually in Michigan. As I mentioned, I did have an aunt and uncle who lived in Arizona, but they were transplants from Michigan, where both my parents grew up. When I was younger, all eight of us would pile into our Buick station wagon, back in the days when the buttons on the radio resembled silver chiclets, and seatbelts were merely a suggestion. Since I was the youngest, I had to sit in the last row, which faced backwards. Can you imagine riding twelve hours backwards? We did enjoy making faces at the cars behind us though.

When I was a kid, all motel rooms had exterior entrances, Shoney's was considered fine dining, and a stop at Stuckeys for rock candy or salt water taffy was the highlight of the trip.

Most of my Michigan relatives lived in farm houses. Real, wood-siding farm houses with porches, barns, tractors and chickens. The thermostats were windows; the cooler you wanted it, the more you would open. Providing sleeping arrangements for eight was always a challenge. Sometimes, half our family slept at one house, and half at another. The younger kids always got the short end of the stick, sleeping four to a bed, or a folding chaise lounge, or on the floor. I never slept on an ironing board, though.

Yes, we will go to great lengths to travel, to see parts of the world different than our own. These trips leave a lasting imprint on our memories as we get older.

For our honeymoon, we went to St. Lucia, a small island in the West Indies. For a southern boy who had never left North America, this was a special trip for me. Yes, it was certainly special to celebrate my marriage and the start of our lives together. But it was also special because I had never been so far from home. I always thought pictures of the Caribbean were altered to make the water look that bright shade of blue. I was wrong. That transparent turquoise water was a sight to behold.

## WHY WORSHIP GOD?

St. Lucia is a treasure chest of natural wonders, from its pristine beaches to its rugged mountains. It comes complete with its own rain forest, banana plantation and active volcano. Our honeymoon was one of my trips of a lifetime, and Kim and I both hope to return.

When I look at my life today, I still possess a spirit of adventure. I think many of us do. What is it that drives us to explore...to see different parts of the country, or even the world? Maybe it's because we get tired of being in our hometowns, so we yearn for a change of scenery. Maybe it's because we know that if we're on vacation, then we are not at work. Maybe it's because there's a lot of cool stuff on this planet that we need to check out, before we check-out.

Have you ever thought about why we have mountains and valleys? Deserts and rain forests? Oceans and lakes? Do you think our world—and its diversity and wonder—was created by accident? I hardly think so. I believe our planet is a gift to all humanity, signed by God. In the first Chapter of Genesis, God gives us the earth:

*"Then God said, 'Let us make mankind in our image, in our likeness, so that they may rule over the fish in the sea and the birds in the sky, over the livestock and all the wild animals, and over all the creatures that move along the ground.'"*

*God blessed them and said to them, "Be fruitful and increase in number; fill the earth and subdue it. Rule over the fish in the sea and the birds in the sky and over every living creature that moves on the ground."*

# The Gift of Earth

*Then God said, "I give you every seed-bearing plant on the face of the whole earth and every tree that has fruit with seed in it. They will be yours for food.* [30] *And to all the beasts of the earth and all the birds in the sky and all the creatures that move along the ground—everything that has the breath of life in it—I give every green plant for food." And it was so.*[1]

Those verses tell me that God has made us managers of the planet. We are free to cultivate it, and we are also free to enjoy it. The earth is like a giant museum, and all the exhibits were designed, built, and carefully placed by God for our enrichment. As I've grown older, I have come to appreciate this place for its natural treasures more and more.

One of the things I love about God's creations is His attention to detail. He doesn't miss a thing.

I used to think of a mountain as a big rock, which had convenient slopes for snow sports, but now I see it as a majestic sculpture whose size baffles the imagination. To think that there is a power who could create something so incredibly large with His bare hands makes me realize how small and powerless I am. To look at how sunlight mixes with rock, earth and plants to create all the shadows and lines makes a mountain a fascination to behold.

A while back, I read this headline: "Could this be God?" Curiosity got the best of me, so I clicked on it. What I saw was a single drop of water, frozen by the camera just as a tiny ripple is created. Look at it. How could something so insignificant—something that happens millions of times each day—be so beautiful? The entire event happens in less than a second. The camera that took that picture literally had one chance to capture the wonder of that droplet of water. After it lands, it's over forever.

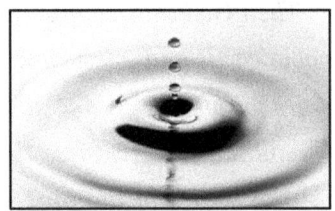

Our family is a beach family. The closest beach is a seven-hour drive, yet we still try to go every year. There is nothing better to me than crossing over that old, gray, sand-covered boardwalk and getting that first glimpse of the ocean each year. The warm salty air; the seagull's constant touch and go between the sand and the sky as they go about their daily routines. And that beautiful water rolling in and out as it does every hour of every day of every year.

The sea stretches as far as the eye can see. The surf can be gentle enough to put you to sleep, or the waves violent enough to sink a ship. A truly awe inspiring sight to me is how the sunlight reflects off the waves of the ocean. Millions upon millions of bright, tiny indentions of light, all moving in harmony with the waves. Only God could give us a detail so subtle, yet so beautiful. I love to get into the ocean; to feel the wetness of the water and the power of the waves, and just think about how creative God is to have given us liquid.

I don't really see the sky as just blue or gray, but rather as the ever changing backdrop of our lives, which so accurately reflects Mother Nature's mood at any given moment. God gives us clouds that can be ominous, reflecting a thousand shades of gray. They can be white and fluffy; coming in momentary shapes that resemble anything from a puppy to honest Abe. They can be those translucent clouds that take the shape of stripes and swirls high in the sky. Our sky can be a flawless shade of brilliant blue, or it can reflect deep hues of pink and purple and orange and red. To call our sky either blue or gray is selling it short. It is always changing; always fascinating.

As the sun goes down, the iris sky darkens to a deep midnight blue, revealing all the stars and planets, which God has hung in place. As humans, we cannot understand the concept of a never-ending universe; that the sky continues forever. To think there are planets and stars a billion light years from us is incomprehensible to my simple mind. But on a clear night, there is nothing better than laying in the grass—or chaise lounge on the patio—and gazing at the thousands of stars that twinkle in the heavens above.

I bought this book not too long ago called *The World's Must-See Destinations; Heaven on Earth*. It was in the check-out line at the grocery store with all the magazines. It is filled with photos from some of the most breathtaking destinations on the planet. There are pictures from places like Katmai National Park in Alaska; Kauai, Hawaii; the Maldives Islands; the Isle of Wight; Krabi, Thailand; and Bora Bora, just to name a few. If you find time, you should look up some of these places. They will give you a small window into this awesome planet God has given us, and may also add a few things to your bucket list.

Countless thousands have dedicated their lives to exploring our beautiful planet. Many have made earth their giant playground. Just recently, there was a story of a 16 year-old girl who attempted to sail around the world. We've heard stories of people attempting to circle the globe in airplanes or hot air balloons, and people who spend their lives ascending the great summits of each continent.

God didn't have to make earth as cool as He did. He could have made it a flat, dusty, boring place. I'm sure you've been on these long, bland stretches of highway before. They make an hour seem like a day. The best drives are the scenic ones; riding along a ridge overlooking the ocean, or seeing the brilliant fall foliage in the New England states. I always loved driving through the mountains and seeing those "steep grade ahead" signs; that means "adventure ahead!" to me. (That's when I wish someone else was driving!) The fact that He crammed Earth with so many wonders is a truly a testament to His love and grace for us.

And the earth provides, too. We must give our planet credit for every resource we have, because everything comes from the earth. The parts that make the television in the corner of your living room were cultivated from the ground. God has given us about 375,000 different species of plants for us to use as food, fuel, and materials. (Trivia time: 20,000 species of plants are edible.)

When I compare God's creations to man's, there is no comparison. A car has about ten thousand parts on it. A single tree has two-hundred thousand leaves on it. It's unusual for a car to last even twenty years without a major overhaul. God's trees last hundreds of years. Even the lifespan of an old primitive human is almost four times as long as a twenty year-old car. And

## The Gift of Earth

God is the only one who can manufacture billions of leaves and blades of grass in just a few weeks each spring.

We have not—nor will we ever—be able to duplicate life, and this includes plants. It's not like Einstein could create a rose bush from some chemicals. We've tried to duplicate body organs and limbs with such limited success. Don't get me wrong; modern medicine has made tremendous advances, and we can keep people alive longer now than ever. It's just that a prosthetic hand is no match for the real thing. All this is just a testament to how all-knowing our Father in heaven really is.

Another testament to God's sheer brilliance lies in the animal kingdom. Talk about attention to detail! To look at the millions of different animals, all unique, and decorated with so many different textures, furs, colors and shapes. It is truly amazing. I would challenge you the next time you watch an animal show—or look at an animal book—or go to the zoo—to think about God when you look at His splendid creatures. Look at His detail and creativity. Look at the raw power in the lions, alligators or elephants, to the delicacy of a butterfly, or the oddity of a blowfish. We are even given animals that live right among us—in our own homes—with the pets we love so much. God has decorated this planet with such a diverse group of living beings, too grand to grasp.

**God's Little Seagull**

A few years ago, Kim and I snuck down to the beach for a long weekend. After a long day of staring at the sea with our feet in the sand, we came back to our condo to get cleaned up for dinner. While Kim was getting ready, I planted myself outside on the balcony, and just gazed at the coastline three floors below. As I was lost in thoughts of nothingness, a seagull appeared beside the balcony. The combination of the ocean breeze and the shape of a seagull's wings will give the illusion that the bird is suspended in flight. For what seemed like an entire, motionless minute, that seagull was completely frozen in thin air. It was like I was looking at a billboard instead a live animal, not five feet from my chair.

As we had our moment together, the only thing I could think of was that God created that bird. He put that bird on this earth, beside my balcony, at the precise moment I was out there. It was all His doing. And why? To fascinate me? To amuse me? To prove once again that He is a God of love, and that little bird was a symbol of it? I'm not really sure, but what I do know is at that very moment, the stack of work on my desk back at the office didn't matter. The disappointment of losing a big sale just the day before was no big deal anymore. The fact that we would have piles of laundry and no groceries when we got home late Sunday, with work and daycare the following day wasn't a concern. For one quiet, special minute, I was at total peace...the kind of peace only God can give. The kind of peace we will one day experience for eternity. And I owe it all to God's little seagull.

I don't know about you, but I try to look at the earth differently these days. I look at its wonders and think only about God. He has provided this wonderful place for all of us to spend a relatively short time before we go to our real home. Is it perfect? Heck no. The sad truth is that it's mainly the humans that cause all the problems. I mean, I didn't have any problems with bears or lions today, but the people at work sure gave me trouble.

Are there natural disasters here? Absolutely. And their purpose boggles my feeble brain. I don't believe that God singles out the evil people to be devastated or killed by a natural disaster. I'm sure many good hearts have been ravaged by them as well. Maybe they are God's way of demonstrating His sheer power, or perhaps a reminder to us all not to get too comfortable here, for this is not our home. Whatever their purpose, it's on my list of questions to ask when I get to heaven. Although I will have no choice but to accept an act of nature's fury, it is not my intention to live in fear of it.

My intention is to focus on the beauty of my earthly habitat while I'm here. And I thank God for that.

# WHY WORSHIP GOD?

# Chapter Eight:
# The Comparison Dilemma

Our local paper features a nice real estate section every Sunday. There is always a story about how some family found the perfect home for their two kids, twelve pets, and ceramic elephant collection. It also includes all property transfers that were registered through the County Property Assessor in recent weeks. This means if you just bought a new home, the price of that home is plastered in black and white for everyone to see in the

## WHY WORSHIP GOD?

Sunday paper. They should probably include a picture of your underwear as well.

I have to admit, I scour the names on those property transfers every week...at least the ones in my zip code. Part of me thinks its wrong, but I just can't help it. If I see the name of someone I know, I instantly know whose house cost more.

When Emma got her new backpack, it launched a debate between her and our seven year-old neighbor Bryson over whose backpack had more zippers. I heard this discussion from the other room. It was somewhat entertaining.

In chapter six, we talked about the gift of intelligence that God gave us. I also talked earlier how original sin instilled some negative emotions in our character. The combination of our superior analytical skills—and the emotion of envy—comes the instinctive habit of comparing ourselves to others. We compare our possessions, our abilities, our looks, our height, weight, shoe sizes...just about everything you can imagine. When the Sunday paper comes out, I rush to the real estate section to see if my peers measure up to me in regard to the size of their mortgage.

For those of you with multiple kids, I'm sure you've been faced with the challenge of making sure each kid gets an equal number of presents at Christmas, or birthdays. We have to make sure there is a level of fairness among each child; that each one is treated equally. If we don't, our kids are usually the first to point out the inequity. I think this is where we get the mentality that, as adults, we are all equally deserving of the same things. If your neighbor gets a new BMW, then you deserve a BMW as well. If

## The Comparison Dilemma

your other neighbor puts in a pool, then you have the right to be pool-worthy too.

This mentality is flawed. Do you remember the section on free will from chapter one? Well, then, you would agree that we are free to choose our careers. Some people choose to be doctors…others (like me) choose to sell insurance. Doctors earn more money than insurance people (at least me anyway), and therefore can more easily afford a Mercedes. This presents a whole new problem with our flawed mentality. Some people who can't really afford a Mercedes buy one anyway to make the world think they are more affluent than they really are. Then they get into financial trouble, which leads to stressed out lives, and sometimes creates problems much greater than that.

God thinks you are wasting your time if you worry about keeping up with the Jones'. In Ecclesiastes 4:4, the author writes, *"And I saw that all labor and achievement spring from man's envy of his neighbor. This too is meaningless, a chasing after the wind."*[1] In Proverbs, we read, *"A heart at peace gives life to the body, but envy rots the bones."*[2]

And all the stuff? God doesn't think much of it either. King Solomon, who was the wisest and wealthiest man of his day, is thought to be the author of the book of Ecclesiastes. In it, he states, *"I also owned more herds and flocks than anyone in Jerusalem before me. I amassed silver and gold for myself, and the treasure of kings and provinces. I acquired men and women singers as well—the delights of the heart of man."* *"I denied myself nothing my eyes desired; I refused my heart no pleasure. Yet, when I surveyed all that my hands* *had done and what I had toiled to achieve, everything was meaningless, a chasing after wind; nothing was gained under the sun."*³

Solomon is saying that every minute spent making money takes away a minute for making memories. The stuff doesn't matter; you cannot take it with you. The book of Timothy states, *"We brought nothing into the world, and we can take nothing out of it."*⁴ It doesn't cost a dime to play a prank on a friend, or to play hide and seek with a kid, or to take a walk with your spouse. We all know the fondest memories are created by people, not possessions.

God never promised equality, either. You can probably think of someone who is a real jerk, yet falls backwards into success. In Matthew, chapter 5, Jesus tells us that God *"causes his sun to rise on the evil and the good, and sends rain on the righteous and the unrighteous."*⁵ You might even know some really good people who can't seem to get a break in life. God reminds us that He doesn't grade on the curve, and there is no relation between one's heart and his or her possessions. *"…righteous men who get what the wicked deserve, and wicked men who get what the righteous deserve. This, too, I say, is meaningless."*⁶ "Whoever dies with the most toys wins" is not truly the objective of life.

The verses above tell us that if our goal in life is to impress our neighbor—that acquiring a bunch of stuff will lead to a fulfilling life—then it is time re-evaluate. If you think that your neighbors are talking about you because of your seven year-old dented vehicle, then you are missing the point. God wants you to appreciate His gifts to you, and not to be envious of your

## The Comparison Dilemma

neighbor's fortunes. Since we are all wired so differently, God works in our lives differently. Comparing your stuff to your neighbors is like comparing an apple to an orange. God deals with each one of us in our own, unique way.

When my wife was a kid, her father ran a small ad agency. His job was to meet with clients, learn all about their specific needs and objectives, and create an ad campaign specifically tailored for that client. No two campaigns were ever alike.

God has created a custom "life campaign" for you, based on your needs and His objectives for you. No two are alike. Some people's life campaigns include blessings of great wealth; others don't. But just because you never become a millionaire doesn't mean you're not blessed in countless other ways. You see, God knows your needs better than you know them. He knows some people are not mature enough to handle the responsibility that comes with great wealth, so He doesn't give it to them. At least not now. God doesn't want to place a level of temptation in front of you that you can't handle. We're talking about eternal consequences here, and God wants to put you in a winning position. It might not seem fair, but living a lavish life here on earth isn't the goal. Rick Warren, author of *The Purpose Driven Life*, put it this way. "God cares more about your character than your comfort." How profound and true that statement is.

I love to throw the "unfair card" when another family gets to go on a fancy vacation that we can't afford, or when I hear of an acquaintance closing a big deal, or getting a promotion at work. That's my envious sin nature at its best, and I hope you can relate. But we've got to trust God's plan for us, and realize that we all receive blessings and we all have challenges. It's just that they aren't all the same.

I have a bad habit at looking at successful people and thinking how lucky they are. But wealth sometimes comes with a high price. A highly paid salesperson who spends four nights on the road each week away from his family. Or the researcher who works eighty hours each week. Or the vice president who lives under an almost unbearable load of stress each day of his life. And, of course, there are careers that are not marriage compatible...many of us know someone whose career cost him or her their marriage. When I was a starry-eyed twenty-something with huge dreams of success, my roommate put it this way: The amount of money a job pays is directly related to how much stress it produces. I think he may have been onto something. To keep things in perspective, I have to remind myself of the downside of wealth, and what people have to endure to achieve it.

Consequently, I know of some families—one in particular with four kids—who live in little three bedroom homes across town, and true happiness and contentment are plastered all over their faces. They are such great people to be around. Happiness is a choice that comes from within. You can be happy under any circumstance if you choose to be. Consequently, you can have it all and never be happy. The choice is ours to make.

How did we become so insecure that we must measure our value by our worth? What's funny is that I don't choose my

## The Comparison Dilemma

friends by their flat screen TVs, zip codes, vehicles or wardrobes...and I would bet they don't care about whether I have these things either. So it's not them as much as it's me. There is a little voice inside me that tells me I must have certain things in order to be accepted. So I constantly worry myself about acquiring things I don't need and can't afford to impress people who I may or may not like.

Truth is, I like things just as much as the next person. I'm probably one of the worst "want-a-holics" out there. God gave Ferdinand Porsche the gift of creating fast cars; He also gave many others the gift of creating some really cool stuff. I don't think that is by mistake. Certain worldly pleasures are part of God's desire for us to live an abundant life. But having a Porsche shouldn't be at God's expense.

I have a simple rule: Ten percent to God, ten percent to me (savings), no credit card debt. I am free to blow the rest. After doing those three things, if I have enough money to buy that Porsche, then I am blessed, as long as I have a true passion for sports cars and I'm not just buying one to show the world how rich I am. We must be honest and pure with our intentions.

There is finite point to this plan I must share: Keep balance in your life. Let me say, if you've been laid off from a good position, and you now have to work two jobs to support your family, then I commend you brother, and I pray your situation changes really soon. But, if you are working seventy hours a week with the goal of earning your *second* million before age forty—and you've never been to your kids dance recital or ball game—then you, my friend, need to re-evaluate. Pursuing excessive wealth at your family's expense is the same as pursuing it at God's expense. If God has given you a spouse and children, then He has given you an obligation that must not be ignored. Your life is out of balance. *"Love the Lord with all your heart, with all your strength, with all your mind and with all your soul."*[7] Live a balanced life. Give equal parts to God, to your family, your work, and your health.

**The House in the Desert**

Our home is fourteen years old. I love the house, and I thank God for it…but after about ten years, things start to break down a little. If you own a house this age I'm sure you can relate. Air conditioners, the roof, appliances. One day I leaned over to pick up a pile of dry cleaning off my closet floor. (Yes, I store my dirty dry cleaning on the floor in my closet…what's the big deal?) I noticed a few of my dress shirts had mildewed. One wall of my closet backs up to the shower in our bathroom. We had a shower pan leak.

The good news is that most of the repairs were covered by insurance. The bad news is that Kim saw this as an opportunity to re-model the whole bathroom…and I never did get the mildew out of those shirts. I'm somewhat handy, so I did the tile work that wasn't covered by insurance, and installed new faucets.

I think a lot of guys will understand what I mean by the 95% rule. That's where we will complete 95% of a project, but somehow never get to 100%. For the bathroom project, I never

## The Comparison Dilemma

nailed the shoe mould back under the cabinets, and when I tried to install a new drain plug in the bathtub, I accidentally put a hole in the PVC drain pipe under the tub, which I have no clue how to fix. I think I'm going to have to call a (gasp!) plumber.

My wife is in a walking boot. It's a long story about a sore ankle. She decided that a piping hot bath would really help that ankle. I happened to walk in just in time to prevent the *second half* of her bath water from leaking through that hole in the drainpipe. I'm not really sure where the first half went. I'm not sure if I want to.

I really did tell her about the hole in the drainpipe...I'm sure of it. It's that "selective hearing" thing that she always accuses *me* of having. Regardless, I emptied the rest of the tub out with a bucket. Then, when she was sitting on the bathroom floor putting her walking boot on she noticed the nails sticking out of the shoe mould under the cabinets. Double whammy! She got me for two unfinished projects in the same day.

I now have a comprehensive "honey-do" list, exposing all of my unfinished projects around the house. In addition, the flower beds were ravaged by the unusually hot summer, the front door is ugly, we've got rotted windows that need replacing...and that is just the front of the house. We haven't even gone inside yet. My wife often refers to our house as "falling apart at the seams." I'm not sure it's that extreme, but I agree we need to do a little work around the place.

Think of your own home. Old or new, big or small, mansion or apartment; I'm sure there are improvements you could make.

# WHY WORSHIP GOD?

Now, imagine taking your entire home—yard, contents, garage, broken drainpipe, seven year-old car and all—and uprooting it. Imagine magically transporting it to the middle of the most remote desert in the world. Nobody around for miles and miles. Can you picture that? Your front yard now consists of dunes as far as the eye can see. Your back yard now consists of dunes as far as the eye can see. The high in the summer is $150°$. The high in the winter is $140°$. Your neighbors are now lizards.

You know, as long as it keeps the cool air inside, it doesn't really matter if your front door is ugly or not anymore. That's because there's nobody around to see it. As long as it still runs, that old heap of a car actually isn't so bad. The label on your clothes becomes insignificant.

Your house, although small and old, suddenly becomes your palace. In fact, you become grateful to God for providing you air conditioning and running water in the middle of a scorching desert. You begin to realize that your life in the desert would be impossible without the blessing of your home and all of its provisions. In this regard, you consider yourself oh-so-blessed by your God, and you begin to look up to Him with a spirit of thanksgiving.

Isn't it funny? Around our neighbors, we are so quick to curse our belongings because they don't measure up. But take the neighbors away, and the magnitude of our blessings quickly comes into focus.

Every night you sit on your porch, and you look up into the crystal clear night sky, almost as if you have a straight line

## The Comparison Dilemma

directly to God. Since there is no cable in the desert, you read your old Bible instead of watching TV. You begin to immerse yourself in God's word. Your attention is no longer focused on impressing anyone, but it is now placed on God and the life He planned for you. You begin to realize that all this chasing after material things and status symbols is meaningless, and that true life begins and ends with God.

Can you see how your perspective changes when you move away from the Jones'? Even though most of our things aren't the most expensive or the finest made, we begin to realize that they are blessings from above when the standard by which we compare them is removed. We are so fortunate to be given the things we have, and our lives would be much more difficult if they were taken away. So, even though we don't have the "it" car or the "it" TV, we should be thankful for the car and TV we do have, because God doesn't have to give them to us.

We had a guest pastor one night at our church. He explained that he was raised by his grandmother in a very humble home. My guess is that they were probably on welfare, or at best, just a little above the poverty line. He and his grandmother lived in a tiny house just outside of downtown in a very poor neighborhood. One night a horrible thunderstorm passed through. High winds, heavy horizontal rain, lightning, tornado sirens. Just awful.

The storm passed, leaving only a light, steady rain, and a small leak in the ceiling. Drip after drip of rainwater found its way slowly, steadily, into a pot on the floor below. At the sight of

# WHY WORSHIP GOD?

this, the grandmother couldn't hold the tears back, and sat down at their tiny kitchen table, put her head in her hands and wept. This preacher, at the time the ten year-old "man of the house," tried to comfort his sobbing grandmother. "It's OK Grandma. I will go up there and fix that roof for you. I will make so it won't leak again."

"I'm not worried about the leak," she cried. "I'm just so thankful for the roof."

Sometimes it takes a leak to bring into focus the blessing of the shelter.

That story makes me feel like the biggest spoiled brat on the planet. God has given me so much, and I just take it for granted. Nothing is good enough for me; I just want more and more.

So, how is your perspective? Are you resentful for your old dented car? Or do you thank God everyday for providing you with transportation? Is driving it a punishment from above, or is it really a blessing given to you by your heavenly Father? At least you have a car...you could have nothing. Are you mad about the one-inch leak in your roof, or thankful for the thousand feet that are dry? Are you jealous of your friend's new phone, or grateful that God has blessed you with a way to communicate? Do you wish you could have lobster too, or just so glad that God has provided chicken? I know personally that my perspective on many things needs to change. When I think about my family and my home, I realize that God blesses me with so much more that I deserve, and I need to be on my knees each day praising Him for His gifts.

## The Comparison Dilemma

How about making today the day we let go of the Jones'? How about today being the day that we cheerfully accept God's provisions for us without getting distracted by this equality thing? To be thankful for what we *do* have instead of being bitter about what we *don't* have? How about today being the day that we measure success by memories, and not by money? By laughter instead of lavishness? By love instead of lifestyle?

For me, it is so easy to get distracted, and I constantly need to go back to my imaginary house in the desert. I can only imagine how much easier my life would be if I kept my focus on God instead of the world. So go ahead. Take that car to the car wash instead of the car lot, then go pick up your family in it and make some memories. And remember to thank God for it.

# WHY WORSHIP GOD?

## Chapter Nine:
# The Gift of Jesus

"And there were shepherds living out in the fields nearby, keeping watch over their flocks at night. A Roman soldier appeared unto them, and they were startled. 'Do not be afraid,' said the soldier. 'I come to bring you news that will be for all the people. Today, in the City of David, a Savior has been born. The infant Son of King Herod and the greatest of his wives, He will rule the nations and bring repentance to all sinners. He will increase the armies of the world and enforce obedience in God's Holy word, and those who refuse to obey will

# WHY WORSHIP GOD?

*face certain torture and death. He has come to save the world! You will find the baby in the King's palace in Jerusalem. Come, follow the star that shines brightly over the palace, bring your gifts to the gate and leave them, for you are not deserving to be in the presence of such royalty.'"*

If you've ever heard the story of Jesus' birth, then you probably know that the story here is not how it happened. Not in the least. Jesus wasn't born to royalty; He was born poor. They didn't even have a room at the Motel 6 for Him. But, doesn't the version here make sense? Wouldn't you think the Son of God and King of the universe would have made a more grandiose entrance than what really happened? That there would be pomp and circumstance, flowing robes and trumpets? A worldwide celebration in honor of the newborn King?

Wouldn't you just assume that Jesus would be brought up in grand luxury, with servants catering to his every need? I can imagine that when Donald Trump visits one of his properties, he enjoys the finest accommodations available. Wouldn't you think the same for Jesus? My gosh, Jesus owns the entire world! The entire universe!

Jesus should have been the heir to King Herod's throne. The Romans and Pharisees would not condemn him; they would bow down to him. The Jewish leaders wouldn't have called for Jesus' execution; Jesus would have called for *theirs*. Isn't this how we would assume royalty is normally treated?

But that is not how it went down. Joseph and Mary were from Nazareth, and they were merely visiting Bethlehem when Jesus was born. Back in those days, only the wealthy rode horses, so they were probably riding a mule or a donkey. Since Mary was so pregnant, Joseph very well could have been walking beside her. They had to travel to Judea to register for the census. A little trivia? Nazareth is about eighty miles from Bethlehem. Experts guess the best donkey-trot to be about twenty miles a day, meaning it took at least four days for them to get there. This doesn't take into account a very pregnant Mary, and the fact that they may have traveled around Samaria, which is right in between the two towns. A journey that takes just over an hour today very well could have taken a week two-thousand years ago.

My fictional account talks about one of the many wives of King Herod being the mother of Jesus. The Bible says Jesus led a sinless life, so it makes sense that He be born of purity. In this regard, a woman in a consummated marriage would not work. Instead, God chose an unwed virgin. If you are female, how would you explain to your fiancé that you are pregnant, and he isn't the father? ("Uh, Joey, we need to talk!") How would that go over? In today's society, that kind of news is more than enough to destroy a relationship. Back then, it was punishable by death. Can you imagine the conversation Mary had with Joseph when she found out she was with child? There had to have been fear, doubt, and probably a huge fight. Joseph agreed to go through with the marriage, probably to keep Mary from getting stoned to death. His plan was to then quietly divorce her. However, an angel came to him in a dream and explained this situation...and it apparently worked. Joseph did stay married to her, and they had other children after Jesus.

So, Joseph took his due-any-day wife on a week long donkey ride, and when they arrived, Mary went into labor. You have to understand that Bethlehem was more or less a suburb of Jerusalem, and there were no rooms available at the inn. I couldn't imagine Bethlehem having more than one hotel, and with everyone in town to register for the census, it was at full capacity.

Think about this. Who on earth would believe that Mary was immaculately conceived with the Son of God? This, I presume, was kept pretty much between Mary and Joseph. They certainly weren't going to use this as an excuse to bump someone from their room at the inn. Mary and Joseph were peasants, and their hometown was a week's journey away. Some theologians argue that Mary and Joseph may have stayed with relatives. The Bible doesn't specifically say where Jesus was born; it just says there was no room at the inn. Why would they go to the inn first, then to a relative's house as a second option? This just doesn't make sense. I like the common idea that Jesus was born in a barn. The Savior of the world, the King of kings, the Son of God…born in a filthy stable.

As a kid, I always thought a manger was an old-fashioned term for a crib. It's not. A manger is a feeding trough. What pigs were eating from earlier that night was now filled with hay and occupied by a newborn. Our modern minds would automatically connect a feeding trough with a farm. You have to remember the period, though. Back in 1 B.C. (or is it 1 A.D.?), everyone had

## The Gift of Jesus

livestock. A manger back then was as common as the home computer is today. This is probably where scholars get the idea that Jesus wasn't necessarily born in a stable.

The details surrounding Jesus' birth don't really matter now, do they? All we know is that He was born in the most humble of circumstances. And this wasn't by accident. This verse in Philippians 2 sums it up well: *"Who, being in very nature God, did not consider equality with God something to be grasped, but made himself nothing, taking the very nature of a servant, being made in human likeness."*[1]

When the light of world was born, the message was clear: If you think that status and stature on this earth matter, you are missing the point. Jesus did not come here to impress people with his riches. On the contrary, He came to teach us how to love. There is a stark contrast between love and stature.

Fast forward thirty-something years later, when Jesus was preaching. He never really catered to the religious leaders of the day. Because of this, I would think that they looked upon Him as a renegade. Although there are thirty-four miracles by Jesus written in the Bible, some of the high priests still doubted that Jesus was the Messiah. In Luke's account of His birth, he didn't write that any angels ascended upon the high priests. No. The angels ascended upon the shepherds in the fields; the common folks.

Jesus spent most of His time with "sinners." You and I are sinners. The guy next door is a sinner. Billy Graham is a sinner. That's not what the Bible is talking about in this context. Back then, "sinner" referred to a person who didn't take God's law seriously. In modern terms, agnostic. Sure, they knew there was a God and that's all fine and good, but they didn't see any real value in honoring His commands. These are the people He hung out with. Why? *"It is not the healthy who need a doctor, but the sick. I have not come to call the righteous, but the sinners."*[2]

You would think that Jesus would have gotten along with the religious leaders; that they could form an alliance to really spread the word of God throughout the land. But, Jesus' spoke of a new way to salvation, which turned the religious world upside-down.

You see, Jesus didn't come to re-hash the Old Testament; God sent Him here to bring us some news. Jesus brought us a message from heaven. In Ephesians chapter two, we read, *"For it is by grace you have been saved, through faith—and this not from yourselves, it is the gift of God—not by works, so that no one can boast."*[3] Jesus' message was that salvation is given to anyone who would simply believe. What great news it was and is! Gospel means "good news."

I've always heard different views of how people got into heaven before Jesus. Original sin separated man from God; it wasn't until Jesus died for our sins that we could be reunited with God. So, it seems to me that getting into heaven before Jesus must have been very difficult. I've heard some say that people had to follow the letter of the law back then, and offer sacrifices for their sins. Others claim that people in the Old Testament days had to believe in the Savior yet-to-come, and this faith would get you into heaven.

## The Gift of Jesus

Either way, Jesus changed the rules. His free offer of salvation, simply by accepting Him as the Savior was contrary to the belief of the Jewish leaders. They thought salvation was only accomplished through acts, and the concept of salvation as a gift wasn't possible. Since Jesus was lukewarm to the leaders of His day at best, many of them didn't believe His claims to be the Son of God.

Imagine an NFL football team who hires a new coach. This new coach comes in and tells the team they are going to completely change their offensive and defensive strategies. They are going to implement a spread offense to replace the pro-set formation they had used for years. On defense, they are going to change from their outdated nickel formation to a forty-six.

This news might not be well received by the veterans who have had success with the old system and are not used to this change. How dare a new coach come in and tell these ten-year veterans what to do? This is their team, and they are going to do things their way. There is going to be doubt and resistance to the new system, which makes the new coach's job much more challenging.

The religious leaders had long believed in salvation through deeds and offerings, so Jesus' teaching of salvation as a gift went against their grain. Just like a new coach wanting to change a system that has been in place for years, Jesus' way was met with resistance. Think of yourself as one of the high priests back in Jesus' day. You begin to hear stories of this young guy, claiming be the Messiah and traveling the countryside like a nomad with this gang of misfits. He is telling the people there is a different way to salvation, and He is performing miracles that no one can explain. After a while, He starts to gain quite a following. As a religious leader, this person is contradicting your core beliefs, and He is starting to get people to turn from your traditional ways. Their thinking was that if they didn't stop Him soon, they were going to have a revolution on their hands. So that's what they did. They nailed Him to a cross. Look at the palm of your hand. Now imagine a spike the size of a pencil through the middle of it.

We had a discussion not long ago about what God is like. It's funny; a lot of people use an "angry God" description, which may fit with the natural disasters and violence in the world. Some think of an old-fashioned God who does not tolerate rule-breaking and seems to be against fun. After all, many sins are fun according to the world view. This is the "outdated God;" the one whose doctrine doesn't fit with our modern lifestyles.

I think if you want to really understand what God is like, look at Jesus. The fruit doesn't fall far from the tree, right? Isn't Jesus God in human form?

When I think of Jesus, I hardly think of a harsh, non-tolerant dictator. When I think of Jesus, I think of the Great Helper, the Great Teacher, the face you would want to see walk through the door at your darkest hour. Jesus is the one person willing to help anybody, including you. He did not come to earth to judge you for your terrible deeds, but rather to help you leave your old life behind. John 3:16 is one of the most widely recognized verses in

## The Gift of Jesus

the Bible, because it really identifies its central theme: *"For God did not send his Son into the world to **condemn** the world, but to save the world through Him."*[4] He didn't come to condemn you for your problems; He came to help you though your problems.

Is God much different? God sent Jesus to earth to reveal Himself to us. He wanted to show us that He is a God of love, forgiveness and mercy. He wanted to show us that He is a God who keeps His word, and who can be trusted to guide you through all areas of your life. Jesus was hardly a God who shot lightning bolts out of His fingers to kill the sinners of the world. If you've never done so, take the time to read the wonderful stories of Jesus in the New Testament. Start with the Gospels of Matthew, Luke, Mark and John.

**Degrees of Sin**

Why? Why are the Gospels the good news, and why is Jesus so important? Why was the birth of Jesus so significant that it even reset the timeline of human history? Because, from the time that Adam and Eve committed the first sin until the birth of Jesus, God and man were separated by sin. Many who died during this time are facing an eternity apart from God, because man cannot save himself.

The Bible says, *"The wages of sin is death."*[5] Not the wages of a thousand sins, but one sin. One lousy sin. Swipe a pack of post-it notes from work, and spend eternity in hell. God doesn't see degrees of sin in the same way we do. We look at a mass murderer and are so thankful we do not possess that kind of demented mind. We are so glad that we are not doomed for the eternal damnation of that person. But, in God's eyes, sin is sin. There are no in-betweens. It is yes or no.

Say a man falls thirty feet from a three-story building and dies. Let's say another man falls thirty-thousand feet from an airplane and dies. Both men fell to their death, and although one fall was a thousand times worse than the other, the end result was the same. To us, murder is a thousand times worse than post-it note theft, but to God, the result is still the same...eternity in hell. In God's eyes, either one of those sins is enough to keep you out of heaven.

Here's the dangerous part. Should the mass murderer one day fall to his knees in repentance of his crime, and confess that the Lord Jesus is his Savior, the Bible says he will go to heaven...just like you. How does that make you feel? To me, it makes me a little mad because I have been a good person all my life and all I've ever done was take a pack of post-its. In this regard, I feel I am *more deserving* of heaven than the mass murderer. God has a word for this emotion. It's called pride, and it's deadly. The minute you start thinking you are more deserving of heaven than someone else, you are headed down the wrong path. No one is deserving of heaven in God's eyes. Just because you can build a house out of Legos does not make you an architect.

We ALL fall short, and we can only get there through the sacrifice of Jesus dying on our behalf. In fact, the murderer may have the edge on you because he has now admitted that there is

# The Gift of Jesus

no way he can get to heaven except through Jesus. The rest of us prideful paper-thieves still think salvation has to do with our deeds.

## The Ladder

Imagine a person who finds himself standing on a big fluffy cloud, just seconds after his earthly death. Out of the clouds rise two boards, about two feet apart, stretching into the sky in a parallel fashion as far as the eye can see, kind of like a vertical railroad track.

The man stands there, confused, when he hears the voice of St. Peter from above. St. Peter explains that the two boards are actually the frame of a ladder, and he is going to give the man one rung for each good deed he did during his life. If the man has earned enough rungs, he is free to climb into heaven. Jesus Himself is the manager of the rung supply.

The man thinks to himself, "This is going to be a breeze. I was a great person while I was on earth." "St. Peter," says the man, "I was a faithful family man my entire life. I worked hard and raised four children."

"Great," said St. Peter. He threw down a ladder rung.

"I went to church every Sunday I could. I was a Deacon in my church."

"That's fantastic," said St. Peter. "A grand accomplishment indeed," and threw down a rung.

The man, standing on the cloud with two rungs on his ladder, yells up to St. Peter. "How many rungs does it take to get up there?"

"'Bout a thousand," he replied.

"Well," said the man, getting a little nervous. "I was never arrested, and didn't kill anyone."

"A bit of a stretch," replied Peter, "but I'll count it." Down flew a rung.

"St. Peter?" said the man.

"Yes…"

"I haven't done nearly enough deeds to get up there on my own. I can only get up there if Jesus would give me the rungs I need."

All of the sudden, THUMP! An entire bundle of rungs came from the sky.

That little story illustrates how salvation is a gift; it cannot be earned. The greatest Christian in the world falls so far short of the greatness of Jesus that the two wouldn't fit on a page the size of Texas. Even our greatest deeds don't measure up to God's standards.

Jesus, God in human form and perfect in nature, is the one person in the history of the earth who truly lived a sin-free life. What He did was take the punishment for our sins on His behalf so we can once again be reunited with God, and have the opportunity to spend eternity with Him. Jesus paid the price. He took the fall for the sins you have and have yet to commit. He paid the price for your grandparents, great-grandparents, your kids and even your unborn great-great grandchildren. He and only He is the way to heaven.

**The First Easter**

Let's go back two-thousand years ago to first century Jerusalem. Jerusalem is about 3,800 feet above sea level, surrounded by deserts and mountains on all sides. The summer months are quite pleasant, with an average temperature of about 75° and low humidity, based on today's averages. If global warming has any merit whatsoever, most summer days would have been in the high 60s or low 70s when Jesus was here. People wore tunics and robes made of linen or wool, and homes were modest structures made of mud bricks with flat roofs. Imagine if you will, being on Calvary hill, just outside the walls of Jerusalem. A mid-day darkness has passed, and you are looking at Jesus, dead on a cross in the bright sunshine.

The media today preys on the personal tragedies of celebrities and athletes. If someone in the public eye is involved in a financial crisis, extra-marital affair, or any other weird behavior, the media pounces. And the public reaction to this news is two-fold: If you are fan of this particular celeb, your reaction will be one of shock, even denial. On the other hand, if you are not a fan, you may be somewhat jovial to learn of this person's fall from grace.

The same thing occurred that day on Calvary. The followers

of Jesus couldn't believe what they were seeing. How can the child of God be dead? Maybe they had doubts about who He really was. "If He was really the child of God, He wouldn't have allowed Himself to be crucified."

The non-believers had an "I-told-you-so" attitude. "What a phony," scoffs the Roman soldier. "Son of God my foot," laughs the high priest. Pilate had a sign made to place on Jesus' cross. It read, "Jesus of Nazareth, the King of the Jews."[6] This made public the charge against Jesus...but it was also a mockery of His claim.

As you stand there on that warm sunny day, looking up at Jesus hanging there against the blue sky He himself created, He looks every bit as human as the criminals on either side of Him. It is looking as if humans have once again wrecked God's master plan of salvation, and the whole thing has turned into a disaster...a total failure. At least for 72 hours.

As we know, on the third day Jesus rose from the dead. The doubts were now reversed. The believer gives a fist-pump and a quiet, "Yessss...I knew it!" while the Roman soldier thinks, "There has got to be a logical explanation for all of this." What looked like a total failure is actually mankind's greatest victory. Jesus took on the sins of the world for all mankind. With His death, the process was complete.

I am a huge sports fan, and my favorite sport is college football. Like many, my favorite team happens to be my Alma Mater; however, we have never been what you would consider a "football powerhouse." In the twenty-plus years I've followed

## The Gift of Jesus

them, we've had two ten-win seasons.

During one of our many down years, we were playing Alabama, the prima donna of college football. To beat the Tide—on their own field—would have been a season-changing event for our team. It was late in the fourth quarter, and we were driving for a score to win the game. As we inched ever closer to the goal line, something pretty significant happened. Time ran out. Game over. There was absolutely nothing we could do after the clock expired to improve, add to, or change the outcome of the game. If one of our guys ran the ball back 100 yards on his hands, it wouldn't have mattered. If the coach agreed to let our team cut the entire field with scissors for just one more play, it wouldn't have happened. It was finished.

Just before Jesus' last breath, He uttered three words: *"It is finished."*[7] What was He talking about? The end of His life as a human? The end of humanity? Nope. When Jesus uttered these final words, He was referring to His dying for our sins. And just like the final score of a football game, there is nothing we can add to change the outcome. No good deeds, no extra credit, not obedience in God's law. None of that matters because Jesus did it for us. The job is finished. The work has been done. All we have to do is accept the gift.

I often think, what did God have to gain by sacrificing His only Son on our behalf? God is completely self-sufficient. He doesn't need anything, including us. Especially an imperfect, sinful race who is doing more to push Him out of our world than to bring Him closer to it. So, why go through all of that? To be humiliated, scorned and crucified by the very people He created? If it were me, I'd be done with all of you...y'all could all rot in hell as far as I'd be concerned. But God thinks differently than me. He gave His Son because He is a God of love. He loves us so much that He wants us with Him. Despite all the bad we have done. Despite the pushback. Despite the disobedience. He loves us that much. He loves you, He loves me. He loves every human on this earth, every human that has ever been born, and every human that will ever be born, and He won't stop at anything to have us join Him!

**Come as You Are**

So Jesus holds out His hand. "Take it," He whispers. "Come with me, and you can live a foolproof life." With Jesus, you can't lose. Sure, you might lose your job. You might lose your house. You might lose loved ones. But you win. *You win! "Come to me, all you who are weary and burdened, and I will give you rest. Take my yoke upon you and learn from me, for I am gentle and humble in heart, and you will find rest for your souls. For my yoke is easy and my burden is light."*[8]

A yoke is a wooden bar used to connect two oxen together at the neck for working...usually to pull a load of some kind. Jesus says His yoke is easy...it is so easy to connect yourself to Jesus; just accept Him as your Lord and Savior. His burden is light. In other words, whatever your load is, it is not too heavy for Jesus. He can handle it. Jesus is telling us that by connecting to Him, there is nothing too heavy for the two of you to handle together.

# The Gift of Jesus

If there is one reason to go to church every Sunday and cheerfully worship God, it's Jesus. He has made approaching the throne possible once again. He hears you whenever you call. And by choosing Him, you are given salvation—eternity with God. And this is not because of us, or anything we could possibly do. It is totally because of God and only because of His love for us.

"I'm not ready" you say. "I've got to clean my act up before I can ask Jesus into my life."

In the Gospel of John, chapter 8, there is a story of a woman who was caught in the act of adultery. They snatched this woman up from wherever she was, and dragged her out into the street. Think about this. The Bible doesn't say which one of them was married, but we know at least one of them was, if not both. One minute, this woman is in a very intimate situation with a man; the next minute she was standing in front of Jesus in the warm, blinding sunshine, about to get stoned by an angry mob. The story doesn't say, but she very well could have been completely naked in the middle of that public place when they brought her out.[9]

My question to you is, do you think this woman had any time at all to clean up *her* act before standing in front of the Lord? I hardly think so. This woman needed a Savior at her darkest (and possibly last) hour. Do you know what happened? Jesus told the group that anyone without sin could throw a stone at her. Nobody threw a thing. Nobody could. The whole mob dropped their rocks and walked away. You know what Jesus did? He forgave her, and told her to turn away from her life of sin.[10]

If you are in a place in your life where you need to "clean up your act" before accepting Jesus, then you need Him right now. You see, Jesus is not going to condemn you for what you're doing; He is going to help you *turn away* from it. And don't worry; you are not going to shock Him with whatever vile act you are committing. There is nothing that is going to shock or offend our Lord. He has seen it all. Just like the men in the story who dropped their stones, nobody is without sin. We are all afflicted. That's exactly why God sent Him, to save us from these sins.

**Chip**

One of my peers in the insurance business recently lost his thirty year-old son to leukemia. At the funeral, Chip's friends were invited to come to the podium and say a few words in remembrance of him. Several people came up and said some very heartfelt things about their fallen friend. I must admit, even though I only met Chip once, it was very emotional. One young man came up, noticeably uncomfortable speaking in front of a large group, and said these words: "Chip, I am better and will continue to get better because of you." Without knowing the whole story, I could only make the assumption that Chip had helped out a friend in need, and this was his way of thanking him.

A few weeks later, I spoke with Chip's father. I told him what a beautiful service it was, and how it was such a tribute to Chip

## The Gift of Jesus

that there were so many people there. Chip really had a positive impact on so many lives. I had to ask about the kid who made that statement though. Chip's dad told me that this guy had a horrible drug addiction. He lost his job. His family turned their backs on him. He was out of money, and frankly, out of options. Chip opened his door and welcomed him. According to his Dad, Chip had a no tolerance policy when it came to drugs. Because of this, it was kind of a shock that he took him in. But, Chip basically said, "Look, we'll deal with the drug problem later. Right now, just come in." Chip took the guy in. Chip convinced him to go back to rehab one more time. He helped him find a job. He listened. He cried. Bottom line is that Chip was a true friend to a person who really needed one. The day after Chip's funeral, that kid closed on his first house.

Do you think Chip got a high-five from Jesus Himself when he entered heaven?

I realize "What would Jesus do?" has sort of become cliché these days, but Chip did exactly what Jesus would have done. "Come as you are," he said. "Just come. Trust me when I say I've got your back. We'll work on your problems later, and we'll get through them together." Jesus doesn't need you to be perfect to report to Him. He needs you to report to Him so he can begin the process of making you perfect. It's a slow process, but if you let Him start today, He will get you to "perfect status" by the time you enter heaven's gates!

I remember going through the membership classes at our church several years ago. The question came up, "If I become a

## WHY WORSHIP GOD?

Christian and accept Christ, will I change? Will I lose my friends? Will I become a Bible-thumpin' Jesus-freak?"

In my experience, the answer has been yes and no. Have I changed? Most certainly. I mean, who would have thought ten years ago that I would be pecking out a book about why we should worship God? My morals have changed. I consider God in my actions and ask for His guidance. I quit smoking. I go to church regularly. Yes, I have definitely changed.

Am I still the same ole Matt? In many ways, yes. I like college football. I like beer. I still have the same twisted sense of humor. I still love rock and roll. I get mad and say four-letter words. I have anger and envy. My question is, who doesn't? Christianity doesn't replace humanity. As people, we all have sinned. No one is immune. Far be it from me to think I'm better than anyone because I'm a Christian. I'm just as sorry as the next guy. This is hardly a book about how great I am for being a Christian; it's a book about how great God is for still loving me in spite of how flawed I am. That's why I have little tolerance for "tee-totallers." If someone dares to look down his nose at something I've done, he needs to take a hard look in the mirror. Judgment is God's job, not ours.

That doesn't mean that I won't reach out to someone who doesn't have a relationship with God, or someone who may be headed down the wrong path to share with them the wonderful gift that God has given us. That is spreading the good news, not judging. Some religions refer to it as evangelism or witnessing.

# The Gift of Jesus

The concept of salvation raises an interesting question. Is salvation the result of good deeds, or are good deeds a result of your salvation? In other words, if you are a good person, help others, do the right things and go to church, will that get you into heaven? Or, can I be a lousy person who accepts Jesus, and that change will lead me to do good things?

I think we've answered that question. If you think that being a good guy is going to get you to the Big Dance, you are wrong. Rather, take the gift of salvation offered by Jesus, and see if He doesn't begin tugging at your heart to do something good with your time. Maybe you'll become a Big Brother or Sister to an inner city kid. Maybe you'll volunteer at the senior citizen's home. Maybe coach a kid's sports team. Start a small Bible study group. Maybe you'll quit the sinful habit you've kept secret all these years, or even the habit that is not so great for your health. It will be your salvation that gives you the desire to do these good deeds.

The point is, let Jesus in first. After He's in, He'll do all the re-arranging and toss out any garbage that needs tossing. It may take awhile, too. It may take the rest of your life.

Years ago, I was at a college basketball game where they were giving tickets to ride the new trolley system that had just opened in my town. All you had to do was go to one of the tables outside the arena and get your tickets. You didn't have to pay anything, sign up for anything, or be anybody. These tickets were free to any and all takers. Jesus is making the same offer. "Free ticket to heaven," He's offering. You don't have to do anything or be

# WHY WORSHIP GOD?

anybody. Just accept. And do it now. Your time in the Army begins with boot camp; your marriage begins with a proposal; your time in college begins with registration, and your eternity in heaven begins here on earth. Your relationship with Jesus must begin here. If you wait until you leave this earth, it will be too late.

Once you accept Christ as your Savior, you probably won't hear trumpets or see fireworks, but a slow change will begin. Will you have to change the way you live your life? Maybe. But don't worry about the details…God will handle those. Just trust that what ever change God makes in you will be perfect. By accepting Christ, you will be joining the winning team, and victory is guaranteed!

And I thank God for that.

Chapter Ten:

# Heaven's Boot Camp

How was your day today? Encounter any problems? My guess would be yes. Hardly a day goes by that we don't encounter some kind of setback. You miss a project deadline because of a sick child; late for an appointment because of traffic; the gas grill runs out of propane and the burgers are only halfway done. It's frustrating. And those are what I would call "daily inconveniences." They don't compare to some of the devastating health, relational and financial problems some of us are enduring.

In chapter one, we talked about how our imperfect, fallen world has a lot to do with the problems we face every day. But, in God's book, nothing happens by mistake. Is there a purpose to the problems we face each day?

**Heaven's Boot Camp**

A new recruit's first ten weeks in the army are spent in Basic Training, or boot camp, as most people call it. These first weeks in a soldier's career are tough by design. The drill sergeants put these young men and women through a grueling regimen designed to test their physical and mental limits. They rise at 5:00 am and spend their days in callisthenic and combat training exercises that make them question their decision to enter the military. After the initial ten weeks, they report to advanced training, where life gets a little easier. Finally, they graduate and begin their ranks as privates in the U.S. Army.

There are no surprises with boot camp. Hundreds of thousands of people have been through it, so it's no secret how tough it is. So, why do so many subject themselves to it? Granted, some do it because their parents tell 'em it's the army or the streets. But the majority enlist voluntarily. Why would they do it, knowing the torture that boot camp entails? Because to them, boot camp is a small price to pay to one day be a member of the United States Army. They know that the suffering of boot camp is only temporary.

You know, life here is like boot camp in a way. Earth is

## Heaven's Boot Camp

heaven's boot camp. If we know that one day we will be promoted to a place where earthly struggles don't exist, it makes life here just a little more tolerable. Yes, heaven's boot camp is tough. It's not fair sometimes. There will be pain. Problems everyday. I think some of life's problems are calisthenics for your character. God throws them down to see if you will respond in a way that is pleasing to Him. If you can approach life here as heaven's boot camp—that sometimes life's problems are divine tests—you may begin to view them in a different way.

**Twenty-four Years of Problems**

It takes twenty-four years of education to become a doctor. The first thirteen encompass kindergarten through high school. You then have four years undergraduate, four years medical, and three years of internship. And what is one of the key educational tools in learning to become a doctor (or anything for that matter)? Problem solving. When you sit in class, the teacher gives you problems to solve. When class ends, the teacher gives you problems to take home and solve. (These homework problems lead to an entirely different set of problems if you don't do them at home like you're supposed to.) Maddie came home today with twenty math problems to solve tonight. She comes home with a backpack full of problems most everyday.

How is all this problem solving measured? By giving us more problems in the form of a test. The better you are at solving them, the better grades you are going to make. Once you've solved all the problems necessary to become a doctor (or whatever it is you want to become), you get rewarded with a degree which tells the world that you are an expert problem-solver in your field.

And this whole problem solving thing isn't limited to school. You have to take tests in your career, to get a driver's license, for fun. The whole premise of most games and game shows is to solve problems.

The point I'm trying to make here is that problems aren't all bad, or at least their purpose in life isn't. Doesn't it stand to reason that if problems are a key educational tool in school, aren't life's problems a key educational tool in life? God puts roadblocks in our way to help us learn, and to help us grow in our faith.

Do you know what the biggest difference is between the problems in school and problems in life? The problems in school are predictable. When the teacher announces there will be a test on chapters fourteen through sixteen next Tuesday, you know exactly when the problems associated with those chapters are going to occur. You will have ample opportunity to prepare for them…and if you don't, you can't say you weren't warned. I guess the only exception is the pop quiz. Pop quizzes reflect life's problems more accurately.

Like the pop quiz, life's problems are unpredictable. Nobody is going to tell you that your washing machine is going to break next Saturday at 9:12 a.m. Nobody is going to give you a heads up that your kid is going to get strep throat on the 20th.

Life's problems come without warning. We had a repairman over to look at our heater a few Decembers ago. I remember hanging Christmas lights outside when he found me and gave me the news: $1,200 for a new unit. Hmmmm…Christmas presents, or a heater? I don't think there is ever a good time to have a problem, but I can sure think of the absolute worst times…and that heater breaking was one of them.

If you think about it, problems can only come from three places—man, Satan, and God. You and you alone control how fast you drive that car, so don't blame God if you get a speeding ticket. If anything, blame Satan. He very well could have been tempting you with the thrill of speed and the excitement of being an outlaw; that is if going ten over makes you an outlaw.

Regardless of their origin, the Bible tells us that we endure trials for a reason. James 1 says, *"Consider it pure joy, my brothers, whenever you face trials of many kinds, because you know that the testing of your faith develops perseverance."*[1] Come again? The Bible says I'm supposed to *happy* when I encounter problems? "Honey, I got laid off today. Isn't that wonderful news?!" In a sense, yes.

The above verse tells me that problems are not just random by-products of life on earth, but rather intentional occurrences that serve a purpose. And even when Satan and the free will of others is the cause of our problems, God has the magical ability to create something good from it. He knows that when we persevere through these trials, we move a step closer to being the people He wants us to be. It is reassuring to know that God cares enough to want me to become better.

Our pastor always says the question to ask when trials come is not "Why, God?" but "What God? What are you trying to teach me here?" There is another great verse that ties into this perfectly. Continuing in James 1:5, "*If any of you lacks **wisdom**, he should ask God, who gives generously to all without finding fault, and it will be given to him.*"² God will gladly tell you exactly what He is trying to teach you with the problems in your life. All you have to do is ask.

I pride myself on being a self-proclaimed "problem expert." Not getting out of them, mind you, but how to get into them. Pastor Craig also made an observation once that it is much easier to create problems than it is to solve them. It's much easier to get *into* debt than to get *out* of it. It's easier to *gain* weight then *lose* it. We get *into* trouble much easier than we get *out* of it. It is much easier to get *into* a relationship than to get *out* of one. Kind of makes sense when you stop and think about it.

My failed business venture racked up thousands of dollars of debt, which we are still paying off, slowly but surely. I prayed for God to bail me out, to give me the winning lottery ticket or an inheritance from a long lost relative. But He didn't. Why? Because He wants me to learn from my mistakes. If He just bailed me out of this mess, I would more than likely do it again. Would that do any good? He loves me, and His lessons are designed to help me in the long run, even if it's tough right now. God wants me to pay my debts slowly to help me learn *not to do it again*. And I certainly get the message! What's funny about this is that there is enough money to make that debt payment every month, in addition to our living expenses. Although God isn't giving me the instant relief I would like, He is providing me the resources I need to get through this chapter in my life, and I am thankful for that.

Earlier in the book, we talked about how God lets us choose our actions. I hear stories all the time about how people get themselves in trouble, then blame God for their woes. A person who is constantly late for work—when he's not calling in sick—and gets fired. The one who runs up her credit cards with careless spending, and ends up in collections. The man who ignores his doctor's advice to quit smoking and ends up with cancer.

Instead of accepting responsibility for their actions, they blame God. "Why God? Why me?!" Remember, God freely gives wisdom to anyone who asks, so I don't think its fair to blame God for things that we bring on ourselves. Isn't it common sense to show up for work on time? Financial experts have talked for years about the ramifications of credit card debt. The dangers of smoking are printed right on the cigarette package. We should accept responsibility for the problems we bring upon ourselves.

Whether your problems are the result of the fallen world in which we live, your own bone-headed mistakes, or life lessons from God, there are some encouraging thoughts about problems.

**Problems affect everyone**

I know I have a tendency to look at the well-kept exteriors of others and instantly believe that their lives are perfect. But they aren't. No one lives a problem-free life, regardless of the polished image they like to show the world.

Kim and I had dinner with a couple a while back, and the four of us really hit it off. We joked and laughed like we were old friends, and I felt like we had met a couple who really had their act together. It wasn't a month later that I learned they were separated and getting a divorce. Do you think they went from happily married—to separated—in the month following our dinner? Of course not. The problems they were facing had probably been brewing for years. They just hid them behind cheery smiles and positive demeanors for their time with us.

**Christians endure just as many trials as non-Christians**

Earlier, I talked about this verse from Ecclesiastes: *"Righteous men who get what the wicked deserve, and wicked men who get what the righteous deserve."*[3] There are going to be trials in your life that you will find unfair, based on the good person you are. But problems do not play favorites. We all go through seasons. You probably know some people who are going through some tough times right now. I'm sure you know some folks who are going through some really good times right now. There are going to be chapters in all our lives filled with joy, and chapters filled with sadness; it's just a part of life here on earth. And it doesn't matter if you're Christian, Jewish, Buddhist or just plan goofy; it doesn't matter if you are as sweet as Aunt Bee or as grumpy as Scrooge, problems will affect all of us at one time or another.

**Problems aren't necessarily punishment**

In John 9, there is a story about a man who had been born

blind. Jesus' disciples asked Him if the blindness was caused by the sins of the man or his parents. Jesus replied, *"Neither this man nor his parents sinned, but this happened so that the work of God might be displayed in his life."*[4]

Just because you encounter problems in life doesn't mean that God is punishing you or doesn't like you. God will use the trials in life to teach, but sometimes He uses them to glorify Himself.

I remember a news story from last year about a baby who was hit by a train. The stroller rolled off a railway platform and onto the tracks. This was a problem the child's mother had absolutely no control over, yet the baby survived with barely a scratch. There is no other feasible explanation other than the power of God at work.

**Most problems are temporary**

Yes, I understand that some of us face ailments and situations that stay with us for life. But, the majority of our trials are temporary. We go through seasons.

Right now, Maddie is in middle school and Emma is in kindergarten. Just yesterday they were in diapers, and the day before they didn't exist. One day they'll be college graduates (at least they better be) with places of their own. When this happens, life will be much different, both for them and us. I certainly won't have to wash Emma's hair anymore, and she won't have to go to bed at 8:00 either. The "Maddie Taxi" will be out of business, and the never-ending trips to whatever practice or function she is attending will no longer be necessary. The girl's rooms will become guest rooms, and instead of wondering when they are going to move out, Kim and I will be left wondering when they are going to come back for a visit. Seasons.

Most of our problems are the same way. Maddie's broken arm and sinus surgery are water under the bridge. Emma's pyloric stenosis and clogged tear duct are cured. My wife was married once before me. At the time, her divorce was a major life event. But today, it is four or five chapters back. I couldn't even name the crisis at work last year which caused me to lose sleep, but I'm sure there was one. Probably a few…

If you could name the major crisis of each year for the last ten years, could you do it? I'm sure that there are some major life events you could name, but could you name ten years worth? Truth is, most of the day to day irritations we endure are forgotten as quickly as they come. "This too shall pass" is not a Bible verse, but in the book of Job it says, *"You will surely forget your troubles, recalling it only as waters gone by."*[5] In 2 Corinthians we read, *"For our light and momentary troubles are achieving for us an eternal glory that far outweighs them all."*[6]

In Christian circles, you often hear people talk about their "walk with God," or their "journey through faith." Did you notice the verbs in those phrases, "walk" and "journey?" God doesn't keep us in one place very long. We are constantly moving; things are constantly changing. Everything is temporary here, including our problems. So, if you are going through some tough times right now, you can rest knowing they will get better. This is merely a valley that you are walking through…Psalm 23 doesn't read "though I'm *stuck* in the valley of the shadow of death." No, you are *walking* through the valley, and one day you will be out of it...so hang in there[7].

**God may have something better for you**

I'm now an old married dude, but recently one of my younger single friends and his girlfriend of two years broke up. It's been so long since I've felt the raw emotion that comes from a severed relationship, I'd forgotten how painful it can be. But the truth is, I failed at every single relationship I was in before Kim. That gives me a failure rate somewhere in the high ninety-percent range. I like to think that each one of those failures taught me just a little more about how to make my relationship with Kim a success. Had it not been for those failed relationships, I never would have met her either. I didn't know at the time that God had something better for me.

I remember getting laid off from a job about ten years ago. At the time, I was crushed, and nervous about an uncertain future. Shortly after, I found a job, which—not only did I enjoy more—but paid more than the job I lost. We cannot see it when it happens, but sometimes trials mean that God has got something *better* in store for us. We just have to keep the faith.

**Our problems help us grow**

If you were to take a survey and ask when people grew the most in their Christian faith, what do you think the answer would be? During the good times? Do we grow in faith when

# WHY WORSHIP GOD?

our children are in honors classes, or when we renew our marriage vows, or when we get a big raise? I would like to believe that I would be thankful to God during these good times, but I would hardly call them "Christian growth spurts." I think that the overwhelming majority of the respondents would agree that we grow the most spiritually during the tough times.

As I mentioned in the previous chapter, one of my peers in the insurance business lost his son to cancer this year. At the funeral, they showed a video the son made of himself right after his diagnosis five years earlier. What was he doing in this video? Clutching a Bible and reading verses from it. I do not know Chip's religious background. He could have been the most devout Christian who ever lived, or a total atheist. The point is, the first place he turned when learning of his terminal illness was God. God gave him the courage to fight his illness for five years before finally being called home.

If any kind of medical emergency arises within our small Bible study group, each member immediately gets an email entitled "Prayer Request." Even during the financial crisis of my failed business, I talked to God, studied God and felt closer to God than ever before.

CS Lewis, a renowned author and theologian, once said that "God whispers to us through our pleasures, but shouts through our pains." Could it be that God is trying to get your attention through your trials? I don't think there is any question about it. God uses problems in our lives to help us align—or re-align—with Him. Sometimes we find ourselves with our back against the wall with no where to turn. And when we've exhausted all of

## Heaven's Boot Camp

our earthly options, our only option becomes God. It is when we sincerely approach God and ask for His help that we begin to truly trust Him. This is when we grow the most.

Are you in this boat? Are you facing a crisis with no where to turn? Have you used up all your earthly options? Well, call out to Jesus. Sit down and explain to Him exactly what is going on, and ask for His help. Say something like:

"Dear Jesus, It's me (put your name here). I've come across a problem that is bigger than me, and I cannot solve it alone. I need your help. My problem is (insert your problem here—take as long as you want). I humbly ask for your wisdom and direction to guide me out of this problem. I pray that you will lift this burden from me. In Jesus' name, Amen."

I think Jesus would reply something like this:

"Hello (your name here). Thank you for contacting me about (your problem here). You have come to the right place. I happen to be the most universally renowned expert at solving this type of problem. Your request has been granted. Starting at this very moment, you and I have teamed up, and we are going to begin working through this dilemma. Wow, this is a doozy, too…how did you get yourself in this mess? I guess it doesn't matter now. There's no need to worry about it any further. And you are going to like my price. I don't charge anything, at least not monetarily. I don't really bill by the hour."

"There are, however, a few things you should know. First, my methods are sometimes unconventional. We may go in a direction you never would have considered…in fact, it might not make sense at all to you. But, trust Me on this one, (your name here). I've solved this problem thousands of times before and I know what I'm doing."

"Secondly, you are going to have to be patient. I understand that when your clock completes two circles, that's a day to you. But my clock runs differently. It took you a while to get into this mess, and it's going to take you a while to get out of it. So, if the process doesn't go as quickly as you would like, then I apologize. But, you've got to trust Me."

"Finally, solving your problem may take some sacrifice on your part. In fact, it might be downright uncomfortable...even painful. I'll try to make it as easy as possible on you, but not only do I want to get you out of this mess, I want to make sure you learn how not to ever get back into it. Hey, no pain, no gain, right?"

"If you are willing to agree to my conditions, we can get started. Just remember, trust Me on this one. Trust Me on every one for that matter. I promise, if you trust Me, I will not let you down. Maybe if I do a great job solving this problem for you, you'll give Me the opportunity to solve others. It's kind of my specialty. You should also know that I do not have a minimum size requirement on my problem solving services. There is no problem too small for you to bring to Me...I'll take them all. Once I helped a kid who put batteries in his toy the wrong way. He asked, so I helped."

"Thank you for contacting Me today; I was so glad to hear from you. You can talk to Me anytime. I'm never to busy to listen to you!"

God kind of has a rule. He wants you to come to Him with everything. And He needs to be the center of your plan of action instead of your last resort. Jesus doesn't want to be a number on your list of possible solutions, like pulling the battery out of your cell phone for one minute, or re-booting your computer when it locks up. Christian author and pastor Max Lucado once wrote, "If Jesus is just another option, then He's really no option at all." In other words, if you can't trust God with everything, then, can you trust Him with anything? This is an all-or-none God we have, and neither of us should have it any other way.

I must let you in on a secret. I think my wife knows this, but honey, if you are learning this for the first time by reading this book, then I apologize. Here's my secret: Sometimes, Kim calls too much during the day. I'm a once-a-day, maybe twice-a-day kinda guy. Six or eight calls is overload. Now, I know couples who talk every thirty minutes—which is fine. It's just not for me. In her defense, it doesn't happen everyday. It's usually when something out of the ordinary is happening, like when the air conditioner repairman is at our house. When this happens, and I can't be there, she'll call every five minutes. "Hi Matt, it's me. He said the outside unit is dirty. You said to call if he ever said the outside unit was dirty." Five minutes later: "He says the condenser is bad. Do air conditioners even have condensers? I thought condensers were on refrigerators. I just don't know…" She'll even text me, just to mix it up. "HE CAN REPLC FLTRS FOR $12. OK??? LUV U." My response: OMG! (The G stands for goodness, by the way.) WUD U LET ME WRK??

## WHY WORSHIP GOD?

I really cannot say that I'm much better sometimes. If I have to do something she normally handles, I'm the same way. If I have to go to the grocery store, I'm the one calling her a hundred times. "Hi Kim? It's me. Did you say fat-free, or low-fat? Can I get generic, or do we need name brand for cheese? Sorry! I didn't know you could tile a backsplash with fat-free generic cheese slices!" Five minutes later: "Do I get the Scooby-Doo yogurt, or iCarly? We use Hunts ketchup, right? Or is it Heinz? They both start with 'H' so it's very confusing."

Jesus is not like that. Did you know that you can call Jesus a hundred times a day and He won't mind? A thousand? There is no problem too small, no detail too mundane for Him. In fact, He wants you to talk to Him. It's His job. He gets irritated when you *don't* talk to Him. Peter doesn't say *"Cast a little of your anxiety on Him,"* or *"Cast up to fifty percent of your anxiety on Him."* He says, *"Cast **ALL** your anxiety on Him, because He cares for you."*[8]

### The Problem Transfer

You probably know how to cast a fishing line. Hold it back, give it a fling, and cast that bait as far as it will go. Jesus wants you to cast your problems up to Him. Fling them as far as you can. He will catch them and handle them for you. I call it problem-transfer. Take your problems and transfer them to Jesus.

The other day, Kim told me the toilet wouldn't stop running. It is now up to me to go to Home Depot, buy a toilet repair kit and fix the problem. It is no longer Kim's problem to deal with.

## Heaven's Boot Camp

She transferred it to me and is now free to forget about it.

Maddie comes home from school and needs a poster board for a project. We don't have one. With her announcement of needing the poster board, the burden of going to the store and getting one now rests on Kim or me. Maddie has transferred the problem to us and can now forget about it. You can do the same thing. Transfer your cares to the Lord and let Him handle them.

So, the next time a problem arises—and I guarantee it will—are you going to freak out and think that God hates you and only wants you to suffer? Or, will you laugh and tell God you are onto Him; that you know He has hidden a lesson in each dilemma that comes your way? When trials come, ask God for the solution, but more importantly, meditate on the lesson. I find it funny that, somehow or another, the problem always gets solved, yet I rarely focus letting the problem improve me. If I can't learn from God's lessons, He may just make me go through them again until His message gets through this thick skull of mine.

Are you ready? Ready to hand off your problems to the worlds greatest problem solver, your secret weapon in surviving heaven's boot camp? It's not as easy as it sounds. It takes practice. Discipline. It takes a relationship. Go ahead. If you've never given a problem to Jesus to handle for you, give Him one and see how he does. It'll change your life. And then thank Him for it.

# WHY WORSHIP GOD?

## Chapter Eleven:
## Not to Worry

Are you a worrier? My mother is the all-time worrying champion. Weekday worrier, weekend worrier...she's the best. She is self-proclaimed. She will admit that she worries excessively. She keeps a worry inventory; a wide range of topics she can pull off the shelf and stew over whenever she needs to.

When I bought my first house, she thought it was too expensive. When I got engaged, she didn't think we dated long enough. She is convinced that at any given moment, one of her children (we are all in our 40's and 50's) will be laid off from his or her job and have to move back home. I was the last one to move out—twenty years ago mind you—yet her door is open for one of us to move back home because we can't hack it on our own.

After finishing college in May, 1990, I moved to Memphis. At the time, a scientist by the name of Iben Browning predicted that a major earthquake was going to strike an area in Arkansas, about seventy miles away. That's where the New Madrid fault line is located, and it caused a series of devastating earthquakes in the early 1800s. Reelfoot Lake, just north of Memphis, was created when the Mississippi River flowed backwards to fill it after one of these quakes.

Browning made a prediction that a major earthquake would occur on December 2nd or 3rd, of 1990. You would not believe the chaos this created in our part of the country. People were upping their insurance, stocking up on essentials like canned goods, water and batteries. I remember stories of people taking pictures off their walls and emptying cabinets. This prediction had a lot of people worried.

Now, if this is how the public felt about Browning's prediction, can you imagine how Browning himself felt? I understand that sometimes people do things for the hype, but what if this man was truly convinced that an earthquake was going to strike? Did the thought of this pending disaster worry him to the point of creating a regional disturbance? Did he sleep

## Not to Worry

at night? Could he eat? Could he focus his attention for any length of time on a topic other than earthquakes?

Ultimately, legitimate seismologists concluded that there was no scientific basis for his prediction. And the prediction that turned a region of the country upside-down for several weeks never happened. Twenty years later and it still hasn't happened.

Most of the stuff we worry about never does happen.

If you google worry, you'll get around 108 million results. Wikipedia defines worry as "an emotion in which a person feels anxious or concerned about a real or imagined issue..." Worrying doesn't prevent, cure, alter or diminish the outcome of any event. With that said, worry is simply a waste of time, and it wreaks havoc on our mental state and takes away our piece of mind.

So, why do we worry? Why do we keep ourselves up at night and deprive ourselves of joy, dwelling on the worst possible outcome? In the last chapter, we talked about giving our problems to God; "casting" them upon the Lord.

The imagery associated with giving our problems away is an encouragement and a comfort to me. I used a fishing example, where we cast our worries to God, much like casting out a fishing line. You know, the equipment used for fishing is not a rod and caster...it's a rod and reel. You cast your line out as far as you can, then reel it back in. The reeling is especially important if you actually hook a fish, because that's how you pull it toward you. That's why my fishing illustration might not be the best one to use in this situation. People will get the mental picture of casting their problems to Jesus, and then reeling them back in. That's not what He wants! He wants you to cast them to Him and let them go (maybe a sling-shot would have made a better illustration). But, it's human nature to reel them back in. That reel is what worry is. Worry is the inability to let our problems go.

What does the Bible teach us about worry? In Matthew, Chapter 6, Jesus Himself put it very clearly:

*"Therefore I tell you, do not worry about your life, what you will eat or drink; or about your body, what you will wear. Is not life more important than food, and the body more important than clothes? Look at the birds of the air; they do not sow or reap or store away in barns, and yet your heavenly Father feeds them. Are you not much more valuable than they? Who of you by worrying can add a single hour to his life?"*[1]

Jesus makes it very clear that, as humans, we were not designed to carry the burden of worry. He tells us it is not healthy, nor does it serve a purpose. He says birds do not grow vegetable gardens, nor do they have pantries in their nests. Have you ever seen a skinny bird? Have you ever seen a bird starve to death? Of course not! If God will care for the birds, won't He also care for us?

Continuing this passage from Matthew, *"And why do you worry about clothes? See how the lilies of the field grow. They do not labor or spin. Yet I tell you that not even Solomon in all his splendor was dressed like one of these. If that is how God clothes the grass of the field, which is here today and tomorrow is thrown into the fire, will he not much more clothe you, O you of little faith? So do not worry, saying,*

## Not to Worry

*'What shall we eat?' or 'What shall we drink?' or 'What shall we wear?' For the pagans run after all these things, and your heavenly Father knows that you need them. But seek first his kingdom and his righteousness, and all these things will be given to you as well. Therefore do not worry about tomorrow, for tomorrow will worry about itself. Each day has enough trouble of its own."*[2]

I love His example about how God dresses the flowers in the field. How many beautiful flowers grow every season that are never even seen by human eyes? Clothing back in Jesus' day was a little harder to come by than now, but the principal remains true: God will provide for all of your needs, so is there any reason to worry? The verse doesn't say Jesus will satisfy your "wants." "Want" is a different thing. I want a new TV, but I hardly need one. He makes a good jab about how little faith we have, too. Verse 34 is my favorite; Jesus tells us not to worry about the future, because it is guaranteed to contain just as many problems as the present. He wants us to live one day at a time.

Why does God tell us not to worry? The passage above says we should first seek His kingdom and our needs will be met. This tells me that God doesn't want worry to distract us from seeking Him.

When I was in college, I took a course on effective study habits. The premise of the class was to teach us to maximize our studying; to learn and retain more information in less time. One of the keys to effective studying is to turn off the radio, television and phone. Furthermore, you are supposed to study upright at a table or desk, as opposed to the sofa or lying in bed. Why? To eliminate distractions. If you can block out all of this external stimuli, you can more clearly focus on the material you are studying, making it easier to retain the information.

We teach young drivers not to mess with cell phones or the car stereo when driving. Why? These things distract us from driving safely.

God feels the same way about worry. Worry is a divine distraction. It takes our focus off of God. You cannot worry and pray at the same time. What you can do is pray about what you are worried about. Try it. You will see that whatever the problem is will become much smaller.

Worry, simply put, shows God you do not trust Him. That's right. You have a heart-to-heart with the Creator of the universe, sincerely tell Him your problems, and humbly ask Him to take them from you (the casting part). Then, twenty minutes later, you basically say, "Uh-uh...I'm taking them back" (the reeling part). Either God hasn't responded quickly enough (twenty minutes), you didn't see angels flying around you, or you think that God's going to handle the problem in a manner that makes you uncomfortable. So you take them back. You take them back because you want to be in control...not God.

So, what is the trick to not worrying? The trick is trust. If you sincerely and deeply believe that God's will for any situation is in your best interest, then the burden of worry is lifted. You cannot lose.

Emma and I have a game. She stands in front of me, eyes closed, and falls backward. I catch her. Have you ever done this?

## Not to Worry

It's a little scarier than you would think. You must have total trust in the person behind you. Emma knows that if I don't catch her, she is either going to fall right on her tail, or even crack her head open. But she will drop back into my arms every time because she has total trust that I will not let her fall. Do you trust that God won't let you fall?

Learning to trust God can be a difficult thing. The parent or spouse of a young soldier off to war; letting that maniacal teenager loose with a motor vehicle; staring a catastrophic illness in the face. Can we really let go of the large-scale worries? The heavy-duty problems in life are actually what strengthen our trust. When we have no choice but to trust God, then we have no choice but to trust God. If you can learn to do this, you will have no reason to worry again. You can live life without fear. Can you imagine never having to be afraid of anything again? *"If God is for us, who can be against us?"*[3]

As you know, sometimes the outcome isn't going to be what you want. Trusting God does not guarantee the happy ending. But if the outcome is God's divine will, then you are getting the only correct outcome to each problem you place at the foot of the cross. In the book of Romans we read, *"And we know that in all things God works for the good of those who love him, who have been called according to his purpose."*[4] This says the end result will be good. The journey may be tragic, but the end result will be good. The verse says, *"in ALL things;"* it doesn't say *"in all GOOD things."* Sometimes it will take bad things to develop the good outcome. This is where your trust—or faith—will be tested.

When we talk about trusting God through tough times, Jesus gives us an encouraging passage in the Gospel of John: *"Do not let your hearts be troubled. Trust in God; trust in Me."*[5]

Can you imagine the person who is going through a foreclosure, and is at peace with it? The peace of God—which as humans we cannot comprehend—can be ours just by trusting our God with our problems. And yes, someone who is leaving the funeral of a loved one, or facing a divorce, or a grave illness, can begin to find peace—not by turning away from God in their tragedy—but by turning to Him. And I am thankful for that.

## Chapter Twelve:
## Called Up to the Big Leagues

Oh, the rejuvenation of spring! The bright green field, with patches of crab grass, dandelions and wild flowers peppered amongst the blades of baby Bermuda. Freshly cut onion stalks release their familiar aroma into the damp air. Grass clippings stick to the ball as it wobbles across the uneven terrain, wet with morning dew. There is nothing more enchanting to a young man than Spring Training in the world of baseball.

# WHY WORSHIP GOD?

This is the story of Johnny and Josh, two professional baseball players for the 1961 Charleston Senators. The Senators were an AAA ball club, and their Major League affiliate was the Washington Senators.

If you're not familiar with how big-league ball works, let me explain. Most players get to the big league by making their way up through minor league, or farm league teams. Players can start on a single, double or triple-A team, and move through the ranks as their ability improves. Once a young player gets good enough, he gets called up to the major league, where his glory, fame and fortune await. Should a player get injured, or go into a slump, it is possible to be sent back down into the minors until he can get his game back up to a major-league level.

Josh was in his fifth year of minor-league ball when he met Johnny. Johnny was a second-year player who was already at the triple-A level. More impressive than his talent was his contagious passion for the game. Johnny had this captivating charisma about him that his teammates were drawn to. He was a true leader. Everyday he would announce to his teammates, "Boys, today you will knock it out of the park!" Everyday. Even his Mamma said that Johnny has talked about baseball ever since he could talk. He lived it. Ate it. Drank it. Johnny *was* a baseball player.

Johnny would wake up at 5 a.m. everyday to get in an extra two hours of batting and throwing. On most days, he would also practice an extra hour each evening (when there wasn't a game). It showed, too. His batting average was over .340.

## Called Up to the Big Leagues

He made a crude wood figure of a first baseman, with a round hole cut-out where his glove was supposed to be. He would practice for hours trying to throw balls from second base through that hole. Word is, he once threw twenty-one balls in a row through that twelve-inch hole 90 feet away.

Josh, on the other hand, did not possess the raw talent that Johnny had. Don't misunderstand—Josh was good—all players at that level are good. But there are ball players that clearly stand apart from the pack, and Johnny was one of them. He was destined for great things, at least in the world of baseball anyway. Josh was more of an introverted type, and wasn't the loud, enthusiastic soul that Johnny was...which is perfectly fine. In this world there are leaders and followers.

During the course of the season, Josh and Johnny became close friends. They were both from Mississippi, and shared a common love of catfish and Elvis Presley. Josh was married, and Johnny had a girl back in his hometown. They had each other to get through the long, grueling season away from their women, which, after a few months, made baseball a lonely profession.

On the field, Johnny's talents really shined. He was the favorite of all his teammates. As a natural leader, he had the batting average of the entire team up from the prior year. Team errors were down, and they were leading their division. Toward the end of the season, they had a nine game advantage over the second place team, and a wide open shot at the pennant. All of this success could be attributed—at least in part—to Johnny's leadership.

# WHY WORSHIP GOD?

During a late season double header, Josh suffered a broken finger on a line drive hit, and had to be placed on the disabled list for several weeks. Coach Del allowed him to go home for a few days to recuperate.

While at home recovering, Josh read the news in his local paper: Johnny had been called up to the big leagues to play for the Washington Senators! Josh was initially exited about the news, but the more he thought about it, the more depressed he became. Who would he confide in during those long stretches on the road? Who would tell him he was dipping his shoulder too low on his swing? In short, Josh knew he was losing a friend.

When Josh's finger finally recovered, he came back to a completely different team than the one he left. Johnny's presence was missed—not just by Josh—but by everyone. There was a void in the group; a feeling of emptiness. The team struggled those last few weeks of the season. Batting averages fell; team errors went up. They went on a twelve game skid, and lost their possession of first place. By this time, Josh's depression had turned to frustration, and even anger.

Late one night, after dropping a series to Louisville, only Josh and Coach Del were left in the locker room. Josh had already changed and packed his bag, but was nervously pacing around the room, unsuccessfully appearing to look busy.

"Something on your mind, Josh?" uttered Coach.

"No sir," he replied. "Just ready to get to the room and get some sleep." He didn't sound very convincing. There was about thirty seconds of silence before Josh swallowed hard. "He wasn't

## Called Up to the Big Leagues

ready, Coach."

"Come again?" said Coach Del.

"Johnny. He wasn't ready for the big leagues. He's not even twenty yet. He can barely get it over the center field fence."

"Yes, but the big leagues called him," replied the coach. "Sometimes they see things in a player that we can't. It's not our job to question their decision."

Now his words were pouring out a little more freely. Josh fired back, "Why couldn't they just keep him here for two more weeks? We could have won our division if he would have stayed."

Coach Del almost gave Josh a compassionate look. "Listen kid, I know you're frustrated. And you're right. If he could have stayed just five more games, we could have locked our pennant. But, you've got to understand, we are here to serve the big leagues. We wouldn't be here if it weren't for the majors. They need him up there more than we need him down here, so they called him up."

Josh just sat there, staring straight ahead.

"Son, maybe you should look at it through his eyes instead of yours. Aren't we all trying to get called up? Isn't that why we're here? You know, they play in front of *twenty-thousand* fans instead of two-thousand. They fly on airplanes when they play outside their division. They get their own hotel rooms with color television and room service. They make...well, they make a lot of money! Listen, Josh, that boy is home now. You know it and I know it. This is what he was meant to do. We should all be thankful for the time we had with him."

"You know Coach, you make some good points," uttered Josh.

"You're darn right I do!" he enthusiastically replied. "I've been doing this a long time, and I tell you, a talent like Johnny is rare. We need to be happy for him."

"I sure do miss him."

"I know you do, son. I do too. But trust me. There is no place he would rather be. He is exactly where he belongs."

The following year, Josh retired from baseball to help on the family farm after his dad had a stroke, while Johnny and the Washington Senators went to the World Series. They lost in game seven.

Josh and Johnny stayed in touch for a while after Josh's retirement, but they only saw each other face to face one time after their season together, when Josh took his family to a Senators game. After that, all that was left were fond memories of an exciting experience, and a great friend.

**Called Up**

Do you know someone who has been called up? Not moved to a new town, or promoted in his or her job, but called up to heaven? To take coach Del's advice in story, let's look at it from the perspective of the deceased. When a believing Christian dies, he or she wins. The goal is accomplished. They have graduated

## Called Up to the Big Leagues

from heaven's boot camp. And just like Johnny going to the majors, that person is home. Your loved one is where he or she belongs. In John Chapter 14, Jesus says, *"My Father's house has many rooms; if that were not so, would I have told you that I am going there to prepare a place for you?"*[1]

So, you, the person reeling from your loss, can you say it out loud? "_____ is in heaven now. _____ is home now. _____ is just fine. I will see _____ again one day." It hurts to say, but it is so true. Once you say it, you've also got to *believe* it. In your mind, these logical sentences are usually drowned out by your heart screaming about how painful it is to lose someone.

My Dad passed away just a few months ago. I think my siblings would agree that either parent was referred to as "Mom and Dad." Momanddad. You couldn't say one without the other. "Momanddad are coming to town for a visit." "What should we get Momanddad for Christmas this year?" Now, we have to get used to just saying "Mom." It sounds so incomplete. In my life, there was never a Mom without a Dad. That has changed now, and I admit it is hard to get used to. For me, I've got distractions; they are 37, 13 and 6 years old. They can instantly take my focus away from his absence. Mom doesn't have that luxury. Mom cooked for Dad everyday, and at one point, cooked for six kids as well. Now, after 57 years, she no longer has anyone to cook for, no one to care for. And that breaks my heart for her.

After he passed, I would endure periods that almost felt normal, only to be snatched back into the reality that he really is gone. I would get lost in the memories of my life with him; a constant forty-three years of his existence in my world. To think that his book is finished, that no more chapters can be written, is truly a sad and helpless state. I would want so bad just to pick up the phone and talk to him, but that is not possible anymore. To know that his ugly, teal recliner will be empty every time I go to visit Mom is tough to accept. But then I remember where he is. He is in perfect health now, and living a life where pain, sickness and sin don't exist. It is the comfort of that truth that pulls me out of my ditch. Dad is in heaven.

The Bible gives us just a tiny peak into heaven. Philippians tells us *"our citizenship is in heaven."*[2] Timothy writes, *"I have fought the good fight, I have finished the race, I have kept the faith. Now there is in store for me a crown of righteousness, which the Lord, the righteous judge, will award to me on that day."*[3] Revelation says, *"Then I saw a new heaven and a new earth, for the first heaven and the first earth passed away...and I heard a loud voice from the throne saying, 'Now the dwelling of God is with men, and He will live with them...He will wipe every tear from their eyes. There will be no more death or mourning or crying or pain, for the old order of things has passed away.'"*[4] In the Gospel of Luke, Jesus says, *"Today you will be with me in paradise."*[5]

If heaven is such a wonderful place, you would think that no one would fear death...you would think we would welcome it. That's not the case. We fear death because we know so little about heaven. We really don't have much concrete evidence about it. While alive, we are completely isolated from heaven. I've read depictions of heaven being "behind a curtain." I'm not crazy about that illustration. If heaven were behind a curtain, I would find it, and do my best to look behind it. I would cut it with scissors if I had to.

I think a better description of heaven is "paradise hidden." We don't know where heaven is. God will not reveal its location to us. You cannot Mapquest it, you cannot enter its address in your GPS. And aside from stories of how someone spent a few minutes in the afterlife before being resuscitated, no one has ever spent any significant time there and returned to tell about it. I always thought it would be great if God would allow Dateline into heaven, cameras and all, for just a day or two. That way we could get comprehensive report on what it's like. Or maybe if we could just get a webcam in there or something.

But God doesn't allow that. It is part of the faith He wants us to have. He wants us to believe—without seeing it—that our deceased loved ones are truly home, and so much better off with Him. Their suffering is over!

**The Blackout**

It seems like every year there is a story on the news about how a bad winter storm causes a blackout. You may have even been a victim of one of these. For some, the power will be out for days— even weeks. There is no heat, no hot water, and food runs the risk of spoiling. Many of life's conveniences are removed during this crisis; there is no cable t.v., no internet, no microwave oven. I would say that enduring a blackout in the dead of winter is a grueling, stressful experience. It has the potential of becoming

## WHY WORSHIP GOD?

quite dangerous. The victims, huddled around a fireplace in five layers of clothing, are left wondering how long their predicament is going last, and not knowing is probably the worst part.

Then, without warning, the lights pop back on. What was dark seconds before is now light. You hear the rotation of the heater fans as they begin to circulate warm air through the vents of the frigid home. Television, computers and home appliances resume their duties as if nothing happened. When we lose something we have become so accustomed to having, there is a renewed appreciation for it when it returns. In an instant, the situation improves one-thousand percent. It goes from hope*less* to hope*ful*—*dis*couraging to *en*couraging—in a split second.

Do you think something similar happens to the terminally ill when they finally leave this life and pass through heaven's gates? A person, tethered to a hospital bed by needles and hoses, unable to move or speak. Hope of even a walk through the park has long been lost. Loved ones fill the room, tearfully reminiscing the healthy days, when that person could walk and run and work and argue and laugh. As the line on the EKG slowly goes flat, a miracle occurs. While tears are falling, a soul is rising. In a mere second, the needles and tubes disappear. The soul of the deceased is floating freely through space, fully alert, feeling better than they ever have. Gone is the pain of his or her ailment; gone is the stress of being stuck in traffic; gone are the temptations of the world. God has released the person from his suffering and called him up to an eternity of peace with Him. It is a glorious event!

# Called Up to the Big Leagues

I've heard differing views of how old Jesus was when He was crucified, but it seems the most common guess is that He was 33. I find it interesting that many professional athletes—NFL quarterbacks, golfers and baseball players to name a few—enter the prime of their careers in their early thirties. This is the age where maturity, intelligence and natural ability all come together to create the most productive years in a player's career. Isn't it funny that Jesus ascended into heaven in the prime of His earthly life? That the years He preached on this earth were those of His physical and mental peak? I often wonder if this is by design; that our heavenly bodies will resemble that of a thirty-three year-old, strong and vivacious like Jesus was.

My father passed at the age of eighty. He had emphysema, and was on oxygen the last ten years of his life. I cherish the thought of Dad in heaven, not as a frail old man chained to an oxygen tube, but rather the feisty, fit, thirty year-old leader of our family, who I never knew at that age. (He was 37 when I was born.) Heaven is a perfect place. Doesn't it stand to reason that we will have perfect bodies?

**The Marble Jar**

I heard a story years ago about the marble jar. A man calculated the exact number of Saturdays he had left, based on the average life span, and filled a jar with that amount of marbles. Each Saturday he took one of the marbles out of the jar. This was his reminder of how precious time on earth really is, and how he should make the most out of every moment. If he emptied the jar

## WHY WORSHIP GOD?

in his lifetime, anything after that is extra; it means he made it to the "bonus round" of life.

There is something endearing about someone who makes it to the bonus round before passing away. At the funeral, you can reflect on that person, and think, "Wow, what a complete life." That person was really blessed to have lived a full four seasons. Someone who experienced marriage, children, grandchildren and even great-grandchildren. He or she saw modern advances they couldn't imagine. War and peace. Bounty and famine. Sickness and health. Sure, the funeral is sad, but there is a peace associated with someone who completes a full life.

Such is not the case when someone dies before his or her time; a person who goes while his marble jar is still full. The father who dies with three young children, or the young girl who falls victim to cancer before she even saw the joy of graduation or marriage. It is during these times when we begin to second guess ourselves, and wonder if there was anything we could have done differently. Sometimes, we allow thoughts to multiply and we start pointing fingers at those responsible for the care of our lost loved one. Losing a loved one before their time can rip a relationship to shreds, and cause emotional scars that, for some, never heal.

If you've been affected by a situation like this, may I share two concrete facts with you? These two tidbits may not have any impact on the open emotional wound you may be nursing, but I will tell you anyway. Do you remember the discussion in chapter two about how God does not change? Well, God's decision to call someone up to heaven is unchangeable. Departing this world is final and permanent. God will never retract a death on this earth. Nobody has ever come back to life a month or two after his passing because God changed His mind. To know that there is no way we will ever be able to communicate with our loved one again after he or she dies creates such a feeling of helplessness, but there is nothing we can do about it.

It is also important to know that your loved one's passing has been on God's calendar for eternity. God knows the exact time of everyone's death, including yours and mine. He knows when you are going to die, where you are going to die, and how you are going to die.

I say these things because the passing of a life is out of our control and unchangeable. In the end, harboring resentment against someone who may or may not have provided the appropriate care necessary to prolong the life of your loved one is going to do more damage to you than the other person. Because of this, we must find a way to let it go.

When someone dies before his or her time, their victory in Jesus is still certain. They have entered the glorious gates of heaven to begin an eternity of great joy. Who needs prayer and support at a time like this? It is certainly not the deceased; they've got it made. It is the ones left behind that need prayer power. The widow left with children to raise; the parent who says goodbye to a child; the teenager who loses her best friend. And when these tragedies occur, the survivor often faces his or her greatest test of faith. How can God allow things like this to happen? How can He take away a man whom his family depends on so much? Our pastor answered this question quite succinctly one Sunday. He said, "I don't know."

We don't really know why God calls some to heaven before their time. Sure, we can speculate. As humans, aren't we great at theorizing? We can speculate about a fallen world with free will. Sometimes the actions of others cause loss of life, be it intentionally or accidentally.

The Bible is full of references to Satan and illness. In Luke 13, there is a story of a woman who had been *"crippled by a spirit for eighteen years."*[6] In verse 16, Jesus says, *"Then should not this woman, a daughter of Abraham, whom Satan has kept bound for eighteen years, be set free...?"*[7]

Matthew 17:14 speaks of a boy stricken with seizures, and Jesus rebuked the demon who caused them, and healed the boy. Again in Matthew 12, Jesus cures a demon-possessed man who was blind and mute.

The book of Job is about a confrontation between God and Satan. Satan tells God that Job is only faithful because God has blessed him. If God took his blessings, then Job would *"surely curse you to your face."*[8] God placed Job in Satan's hands, and Satan *"afflicted Job with painful sores from the soles of his feet to the top of his head."*[9]

Wouldn't it make sense that sickness be the work of Satan? Sickness brings us down. It makes us question our faith and keeps us from being productive. Sickness will even keep us from going to church. When I'm sick, I'm usually not in the mood to worship God.

Can anything good come from a prolonged illness? In his book, *The Last Lecture*, Randy Pausch considered his cancer a blessing in that it gave him time in advance to prepare for his death. He could tell his wife and children all the things he needed to say, and make all the necessary arrangements to insure their comfort after he died. This cannot be done by someone who suffers an instantaneous death.

Could it be that the ones who die young are the blessed ones? If only perfect people enter heaven, is it possible that these people have reached perfection early?

## A Greater Purpose

Can death serve a greater purpose that only God can see? There is a story of a successful young business owner who loses his new bride in a car accident. He was the one driving. The overwhelming guilt of that day destroyed him. He turned his back on God and found solace in a bottle. He lost his business and severed all ties to his friends and family.

Twenty years later, he found himself working at a car lot, selling Fords. A preacher and his wife were test driving a car, and the three of them were involved in a terrible accident. The preacher's wife was in a coma for weeks. During this time, that man and the preacher became close friends. He came to the hospital every day to visit the preacher and his injured wife. He became a rock for the preacher, who was scared to death at the thought of losing his mate. The man, having been through the same emotions years before, had all the right things to say. It was his wisdom that helped his new friend get through the emotional trauma of that terrible accident. In their exchanges, the man found God. Ultimately, the wife slowly recovered, and that broken man is a Deacon at the preacher's church today.

There was a young girl in our community who died of cancer last year. To see everything she went through is nothing compared to how brave she was through the ordeal. Ultimately, God called her home, leaving so many questioning why things like this have to happen, especially to innocent children. We don't know.

What we do know is that a community pulled together. They put their differences aside to raise money, to offer meals and transportation and prayers. If God has a "prayer radar" in heaven, there was a very bright blip in western Tennessee because of all the prayers that were being said for this young girl.

What if, in this grand outreach to God, just one person found Christ? In all the prayer meetings and testimonials and Bible studies for this child, what if one person accepted Christ as his or her Savior? What if that little girl saved a soul while losing her life? I can almost guarantee her parents would not think that is a fair trade. Not in the least. But, will it seem fair when that child and her family have been reunited ten-thousand years in heaven? Are ten millenniums enough to forget the pain of their time on earth, and admit that it was worth it? The saved soul will be up there too, you know.

## Called Up to the Big Leagues

OK, enough. I could theorize for years about why people die before their time, but the truth is I don't know. Nobody knows. Sometimes life is a color-by-number picture the size of Wyoming. (Wyoming is a perfect rectangle; it would make a great canvas for a painting.) All we see are random patches of colored paint every few miles—it looks like a huge mess. The picture takes a lifetime to finish, and it's not until we look down on it from heaven that we realize these random paint splotches all come together to form a beautiful portrait. What looks like chaos now will be seen much more clearly in our next life. Proverbs 3:5 says, *"Trust in the LORD with all your heart and lean not on your own understanding."*[10] Even God agrees that you will drive yourself nuts trying to make sense out of some of the crazy stuff that happens on earth.

Besides, all the speculation in the world will not bring a loved one back. In the baseball story, Coach Del told young Josh that he wasn't to question the decision of the majors. In the same way, we are here to serve God, and when He calls one of His children to heaven, we have no choice in the matter. Sometimes God knows things we don't.

When we suffer great loss, we must turn to God and not push Him away. We must trust in His divine will and reach out to Him for the strength we need to get through. I encourage you to talk to God. Talk to Him in your mourning and despair and your anger. You can absolutely be angry with God. Let it out! Carry Him with you through the gamut of emotions you are going through, and let His peace seep into your soul and give you comfort. That comfort will grow deeper and deeper with every passing day.

In our grief, we must not forget the victory that our loved one has achieved. We are put on earth to go to heaven. That is the goal. For the believers who leave this earth, we must always remember that they are safe in the House of God, and we will see them again when we get there.

## Chapter Thirteen:
# God's Plan Was Different than Mine

In the beginning of 2006, I left the comfort of a 14-year career in corporate America and took a leap of faith that many dare not try. I started my own business. When someone makes a drastic career change, it's either because they dislike what they do so much they are running from it, or they have such a burning desire to try this new career they are running to it. I was definitely running *to* this. I've always considered myself somewhat entrepreneurial, and experimented with many side ventures through the years. In 2006, the desire to start a business became so strong I felt like I was being called to start it. I took my leap of faith.

God and me starting a business together...what could be better than having the greatest Businessman, Engineer, Designer, Marketer, Salesman in the universe backing me? I mean, with God, I can't fail, right? Everyday I would pray for the success of the business, and wisdom and guidance. Everyday.

I had a little money saved for my venture, plus I took the equity out of my house. This was our seed money. Taking the equity out of our home seemed like a prudent risk as I was going to make it back ten times over when the business hit it big.

I started a business building Adirondack chairs. Maybe you've seen one. It's a low to the ground outdoor chair made from wood slats. They are very popular at the beach. For some reason, I was passionate about this idea; it was my ticket to retirement. I was so excited, not only about the prospect of becoming wealthy, but also about the idea of being the boss and creating a company from nothing. Besides, I had God on my team, right?

The first few months went as planned. I knew it would take time to get the business off the ground and get things rolling, and I had budgeted for it. I must confess now that I was shocked at how much money those first few months cost...everything was almost double what I had planned. But no need to panic. It takes money to make money, I thought to myself.

Over the course of that first year, I experienced my ups and

## God's Plan was Different than Mine

downs with the business. One problem I had was that it took a lot longer to get my manufacturing process established than I had planned. I mean a LOT longer. What I thought would take a few months to establish still wasn't finished after the first year. Without a steady, consistent manufacturing system, it's hard to build chairs at the rate I needed to be profitable, and now money was starting to become an issue. I cashed in mutual funds. Two 401(k) accounts. I started charging up my credit cards. I still prayed every day for wisdom and guidance in making the business successful, but I was starting to have some doubts.

I knew if I could just hang on until the second year, things would turn for the better. With outdoor furniture, sales are seasonal. Orders will start coming in early March and continue through late October. If I could just work extra hard on revising my products, putting together a new product catalog and attend a few trade shows, I would get the orders I needed the following spring to right the ship. I had been praying every day. I knew God would answer.

Sales in the second year greatly improved over the first year; more than double. But we still were falling short of our sales goals. In the meantime, the minimum monthly credit card payments were getting bigger and bigger, and I felt like I was on a treadmill moving faster than I could run. At this point I was becoming ragged. I couldn't sleep at night. There was increased tension at home. Collectors were calling the house. I was even starting to fall behind on my mortgage payments. Just writing about it takes me back to that period of my life, and it gives me an uneasy feeling even today.

## WHY WORSHIP GOD?

I remember getting a call from my wife one morning while I was at my workshop. She asked me to come home for lunch so we could talk. Have you ever gotten a "We need to talk, call?" I don't know about you, but for me, those calls were never about anything pleasant. When I got home, Kim had laid out four statements from four different credit card companies, two with $25,000 balances, and two with $12,000 balances. It's somewhat flattering getting those credit line increases over the years. The credit card company really will let you charge up to the maximum, too. The only problem is, it has to be paid back.

I had been getting cash advances off these cards to keep the business and our household afloat, all without her knowledge. While I was at work, a collector called our house, which sparked her curiosity. It didn't take her long at all to find those statements and add up the balances. $74,000. It was almost like I had been caught having an affair or something. I wasn't cheating on her with another woman, but I was certainly guilty of lying to her. That was the defining moment when I realized I had made the mess of a lifetime. Whereas just two years earlier I was an upwardly mobile young professional with a six-figure income and six figures in savings, I was now completely broke with no where to turn and just over sixty days away from foreclosure.

During that second year, I remember having little panic attacks at the mention of money. My daughter's cheerleading expenses, buying clothes for the kids, birthdays, even invitations to go out to eat with friends just made me sick inside, trying to figure out to how to pay for the novel items I used to take for granted. I remember breathing a sigh of relief when the server at

## God's Plan was Different than Mine

a restaurant came back with my credit card receipt to sign...that meant it got approved! Trying to keep this affluent exterior to the outside world while knowing you are in financial ruin is a very stressful existence.

By the end of the second year, I put the business up for sale. But even after my total financial devastation, I was still determined to make the business work, so I set out on a massive capital campaign. I put together a new business plan, and assembled detailed reports and projections on what it would take to make the business fly. I spent days preparing all this. Once I had my rock solid plan of action completed, I started seeking investors. I put a listing on several business community websites where investors can seek out opportunities. I contacted friends and family and local investment companies. I even ran ads in the local paper. All this was to no avail. Nobody wanted anything to do with the business financially. At this point, I was at the end of my rope.

I was confused about my faith at that time as well. I had prayed every day, and I thought God really knew what I wanted, yet it wasn't happening. I had this belief that God gives us each talents and finds joy when we use our gifts to the fullest. One of my gifts was woodworking, so I really believed that I was doing what God intended. Furthermore, I was doing it honestly. Why would God fail me like this?

In January of 2008, I had become a shell of the enthusiastic entrepreneur I was just two short years earlier. I had lost my life savings, failed my family, and failed myself. I had become a

## WHY WORSHIP GOD?

recluse to my friends, and had very little to say at home as I internalized most of the stress. There was no joy in my life for the most part, as I was overcome with constant worry. I remember waking up around 2 a.m. every night, just staring at the ceiling with thoughts racing through my head. I was sending out resumes with little success, and was really at a loss as to what to do next. Then I got a phone call.

An acquaintance of mine—the guy who replaced me at my old job—called to tell me that he had a great year at the company. They were looking to hire another sales rep, and my name came up. We hadn't spoken in almost two years, and he admitted he had no clue as to how me or my business was, but simply that there was an opening and my name came up. During that ten minute conversation, my eyes welled up with tears. God had thrown me His rope. I will admit that I am not the brightest person when it comes to distinguishing between God's will and my own, but this was a no-brainer.

That same day I had a conversation with his boss. We spoke for about thirty minutes, and that kick-started the hiring process. Six weeks later, I was back at the job I quit two years earlier, in the same office with the same desk. The nails I hung my pictures on were still there. It was almost like I never left. I remember walking into the supply room and seeing cases and cases of copy paper. "Abundance!" I thought to myself after two years of buying paper by the ream.

I am approaching the three-year anniversary of coming back to corporate America, and I'm happy to report that we will finish

## God's Plan was Different than Mine

paying back every penny of our business debts in the next twelve months. This chapter of our lives is just about over. When I look back on my experience as a business-owner and what a financial disaster it was, my first inclination is to ask God why. Why God? Why me, God? Why'd you do this to me, God? I mean, I thought we were partners. Like I mentioned earlier in this book, "why" is the wrong word. "What," not "why," is the question I need to be asking. "What were you trying to teach me God?"

While I had tunnel-vision focused solely on wealth and success, God set out to teach me lessons much more valuable than money.

In looking back, I can see now where the decision to start this business was mine, not Gods. He didn't throw a load of wood down from heaven and tell me to get to work. Not at all. I used my free will to quit my job and attempt this venture. Was it a mistake? In earthly terms, maybe, but with God, remember, NOTHING happens by mistake. There was definitely a purpose and lessons He had in mind for me. And He did it because he loves me.

There were a lot of "almosts" during the two years I had my business. We *almost* went 60 days late on some bills; we *almost* didn't have any money for groceries. We *almost* couldn't pay Maddie's cheerleading dues; we *almost* had the power cut off. (We DID get our cell phones cut-off…twice!) Yes, these things ALMOST happened…but they never DID happen. Just like we discussed earlier in this book, Jesus tells us that God provides. Throughout the course of our financial crisis, God fulfilled ALL of our needs and then some. It's harder to realize this while it is happening; it becomes so clear in retrospect. As tough as it was to me at the time, our financial squeeze was so small compared to the trials that others have to endure; it is almost insignificant.

Isn't it great how the hero always shows up at the perfect moment in the movies? The damsel in distress is tied up, about to get thrown into a vat of lava when our hero suddenly comes out of nowhere and saves the day. He's never too late. He always arrives at just the right moment to save the sweet damsel from the evil clutches of the villain.

Movie heroes aren't the only ones with perfect timing. In the Bible, Peter writes, *"Humble yourselves, therefore, under God's mighty hand, that He may lift you up in due time."*[1] Hebrews, chapter 4 tells us, *"We may receive mercy and find grace to help us in our time of need."*[2] When we seek God's will for our lives, He has the ability to answer our prayers at precisely the right moment. God's timing doesn't always match up with our expectations, but when we learn to trust Him, we find that it is always perfect.

God exemplified His perfect timing with me as well. During the deepest struggles with my business, He always provided at the perfect time. Just when I needed it, I would get a payment in from a customer, or an order would come in. Maybe Kim would get a bonus or we would get our escrow refund. It was always at the right time, too. Never too late, never too early. Just right.

The most important lesson that I took away from this experience is learning to trust God. He was there for my family and me; He did provide when we needed it. We never lost our

## God's Plan was Different than Mine

house; I didn't have to file for bankruptcy. And through it all, the four of us had each other, and no collection agency could ever take that away. Was it an expensive lesson? In earthly terms, yes. In eternal terms, it was worth every penny and then some. Just like in James 1:2, the testing of my faith developed perseverance. I persevered.

My career before and after the business is employee benefits sales. It is structured with a low base salary and high commissions. This is to keep you selling month-in and month-out. Before my business ownership experience, I would get so uptight and type-A about hitting a certain sales quota each month. I would try harder and harder, and if I fell short, I was a miserable bear to be around. That doesn't happen so much anymore. These days I work just as hard, but I have given the worrying part to God. If he wants me to have a great month, so be it. If I had a bad month, so what? I now know that He will meet my needs, and it is not all about how much cash I can make in a month. God does not intend for us to bear the pressure we put on ourselves.

When I look at my frantic effort to take control and find investors for the business, I can honestly say I exhausted every possible avenue I could find...with no success. Then I get this random call from a person I haven't spoken to in years, offering me a job. As much as we like to think we are in control and calling the shots, we are not. The sooner we realize that God is in control, and we relinquish that responsibility to Him, the sooner our lives become much more joyful. As much effort as I exerted trying to control my situation, God's holy will changed everything with the one phone call I got from my friend Dave. How many times does God have to prove Himself to us before we finally realize that is not going to let us let us down?

**Aunt Nellie and the GPS**

A buddy of mine bought a GPS for his Aunt Nellie. Aunt Nellie is 82, never been married, and was faced with the daunting task of driving from Michigan to Bradenton Florida alone last summer to visit her sister. My buddy thought a GPS would be just the gift; simply enter the address, and let the GPS do the rest. They did a couple of test runs; like plugging in the address for the local Wal-Mart and other destinations around town and letting the GPS guide her there. It seemed Aunt Nellie was very comfortable with the device and had a high enough amount of faith in it to let it take her from Michigan to Florida.

On the day of the trip, my buddy told Aunt Nellie, "Just type in the address and let it do the rest." Simple enough. Until she called him from central Ohio, thinking she was lost. Then from Tennessee. Each time she would call and tell him she didn't think it was working right and she was pushing all these buttons on the thing. My friend finally shouted at her, "Quit pushing the buttons and just trust it! It will get you there if you just leave it alone!" The next call came from Bradenton, Florida, where Aunt Nellie arrived safely with the help of her GPS. All was fine until the return trip, when the process started all over again.

The same can be said of our faith. All is fine until it is put to the test. Then the doubts come flooding in. Aunt Nellie was fine

## God's Plan was Different than Mine

letting the GPS guide her to Wal-Mart because she knew where Wal-Mart was. But, when she was forced to rely on a small gadget which she had no idea how or if it worked—in the middle of nowhere—it's easy to see where she would have serious doubts. The signal that tells that GPS what to do is invisible. Sometimes it's hard to have faith in things we cannot see.

When our faith is put to the test...like with my business ownership experience, we have our doubts as well. It is not until we get through the challenging parts of our lives that we realize God keeps His word. And we need these challenges to help us learn that. And just like Aunt Nellie, maybe we should stop pushing all the buttons, get out of the way, and trust God to do his work in our lives.

## Chapter Fourteen
# Finale

**S**o, here is a picture of my kid Emma. On the day this picture was made, she was pulling the fire truck behind her with the help of a few jump ropes she tied together.

On that particular day, Emma was not worried about her 401(k), whether she would graduate with

## WHY WORSHIP GOD?

honors, or how big a house she'll be able to afford one day. Her biggest concern that day was the fire truck tipping over. Every time it did, she had to get off of her bike and put it back on its wheels again. It actually tipped quite a bit, at least while I was out there. How frustrating!

A lot of people envy the life of a child, and who can blame them? Take little Emma here. She is provided shelter, lots of monogrammed "emma gear" to wear, and all the chicken nuggets and mac n' cheese her heart desires. She has parents who will protect her from any stinky neighborhood boys that may try to encroach upon her turf. She also has parents who will do their best to guide her in the right direction, and help her learn from her mistakes when she goes off the tracks, even if it means using the word "no." We will listen to anything she has to say, and offer our support in anyway possible. I would say she is completely provided for. I guess that's why her biggest problem is keeping the fire truck on four wheels. Pretty lucky kid in my book.

Do you think God sees us in the same light? Just as Emma is my child, I am God's child. Just as it's my job to fulfill her needs, it is God's job to fulfill mine. As a child of God, He promises to take care of me and offer me an abundant life, if I will only let Him. He gives me divine guidance to minimize my mistakes, and divine forgiveness when I make them. God truly loves us and wants only the best for us, but sometimes His idea of "best" is different than ours.

What if all of us, for just one day, could truly give all of our

## Finale

trust to Him? To be able to fall backwards into His arms and know that He will catch us? To know that somehow, the problem of the day will always be smaller than God? To know that the surgery on a loved one is going to go exactly the way God wants it to go? To know that somehow, the money will show up to pay that bill?

If we could do this, we could live a life without fear. We could live as carefree as a five year-old playing in the driveway. Would that be enough reason to worship God?

In the beginning of this book, I told you how I was the bitter Christian; standing in church with my hands in my pockets, while those around me showed so much praise. I realize now how wrong I was. It's amazing—if we just change our perspective a little—how God blesses us in so many thousands and thousands of ways. It is practically impossible not to want to fall on our knees and thank Him for these things that He doesn't have to do. God doesn't have to bless us…He wants to bless us. And He does this because He loves us!

I also mentioned in the introduction how I wrote this book for selfish reasons. I set out on a mission to find out for myself exactly what God's role in our lives really is. I learned that it is not to provide a perfect world for us. I believe the trouble in the world dates back to Adam and Eve and the original sin. It was man's choice that created a fallen world, and God is our only refuge when the free will of others causes pain in our lives.

I believe only God has the power to harvest something good from the bad that happens in the world. I believe God wants us

# WHY WORSHIP GOD?

to invite Him into our lives, and to cultivate a relationship with Him. I believe that when we do, and we sincerely ask for His help and guidance in our lives, we receive it. Sometimes it doesn't happen *when* we want it to; sometimes it doesn't end up *how* we want it to. But I believe in God's perfect timing, and I believe He knows far better what is best for me than I do, so I completely trust His will for me in every area of my life. And if the answer doesn't come today, it will come at the perfect time.

I am amazed at God's work. Planet Earth and its animals, plants and natural wonders are awe-inspiring sights to behold, and I believe they are God's gift to humanity. Far beyond our planet lies more wonder and testament to His size and power, which further defines how small we are.

I could go on and on about this personal God who truly cares about us and our lives. I've learned that I can lean on Him in everything, and He is there for me. He is the biggest ally we can have both in this life and the afterlife. And when things don't go as planned down here—when tragedy or illness strikes—when our world is turned upside-down with no plausible explanation why, we have to remember that this life is the beginning of the story and not the end. Like I mentioned earlier, earth is not really our home, and I believe sometimes God reminds us of this through the chaos in the world.

If there is a reason above all others as to why we should worship God, it is Jesus. Our darkest moments on earth will one day be overshadowed by Jesus Christ. All of our sin, tears and pain will be washed clean, because God sent His only Son to die for our sins. God loves us so much that he was willing to send a Savior to take away what we cannot take away ourselves. Because Jesus died for us, we do not have to face an eternal torture away from God. Anyone who chooses will be joined with Him for eternity. And that is the best news you will ever hear, and we should all thank God for it on a daily—hourly—even minute-by-minute basis.

**My Software Parable**

The manuscript for this book was written in a computer program called Microsoft Word. I would say most people with computers are familiar with it. If not, let me just say it is the computer equivalent of a typewriter, except there is no white-out. You can delete and re-write to your hearts content without wasting a single sheet of paper. Furthermore, it formats, autocorrects, and puts red or green squiggly lines under your typos and bad grammar. The software was designed for writing. Whether it's a letter or a two-hundred page book, Microsoft Word will make the task much easier.

For those of you who are familiar with Microsoft Word, I'm sure you know that it's one of four separate programs that are sold together in a package called Microsoft Office. One of these other programs is called Microsoft Excel. Excel is not for writing papers. It is used for math. It is the computer equivalent of a calculator, except it can repeat the same calculation over and over again if you tell it to, so you are not stuck key-punching all night long. It does a lot of other neat things as well, and it's very useful

# WHY WORSHIP GOD?

in the business community.

What's neat about Microsoft Excel is that, although it's used primarily for numerical applications, you can also type words into it. You can capitalize, italicize, punctuate. In essence, I could have written this entire book in Excel if I wanted to, and you the reader wouldn't be able to tell the difference. But it wouldn't have been as easy. You see, Excel wasn't designed for word processing. It doesn't auto format the chapters and paragraphs like Microsoft Word. It doesn't have spell check, or any of the other features that make writing in Word so much easier. Yes, I could have written this entire book in Excel, but that would mean I did it the hard way.

You know, there are people on this earth that choose not to live God's way. Oh sure, they speak English and drive cars and look like you and me, they just don't have God in their lives. They live life the hard way. Do you know anyone like this? Are they wound up just a little too tight? It's sad what they are missing out on, really. They are the people who think their fate is in their own hands. They don't realize that they aren't really in control. To them, a lay-off or stock market crash becomes insurmountable instead of insignificant. Since they won't relinquish control to God, they never enjoy the peace of knowing God is in control. They've never felt the peace associated with prayer; how we can cast our cares upon Jesus. They do not know the joy associated with an answered prayer, either. To them, death is the end, and not the beginning. When a loved one goes, they believe it is final. They do not have the hope of spending eternity with that person.

# Finale

Sure, on the exterior, they can live their lives just like you, but it's not nearly as easy. You see, humans were not designed to live without God. Just like typing a book with the wrong software, a life without God just doesn't line up the way it should; it's always off just a little.

## What's the Worst Thing That Can Happen?

Two boys spent weeks building a soap box derby car. They put four bicycle wheels on it, sanded it down extra smooth and painted it five different colors. They decorated it with decals from the hobby store, and even put a padded seat in the cockpit. Since soap box derby cars don't have motors, one of the boys took an old mailing tube, sealed off one end and stuffed it with a wick and a bunch of gunpowder, which he was able to get from his older brother. He mounted the tube on the back of the car to make it a *"rocket* soap box derby racer."

On the day of the test run, as his buddy was strapped into the cockpit, the boy stood by the car with lighted match, easing ever so closely to the wick on the rocket booster. Just as he was about to ignite the wick, his buddy turned around and said, "Are you sure we need to light that thing? Are you positive it's safe?"

"Sure it's safe," his friend replied. "What's the worst thing that can happen?"

What's the worst thing that can happen? We find ourselves asking this question quite a bit in life.

**A new job:** "What's the worst thing that can happen?"

**A shortcut that's not on the map during your vacation:** "What's the worst thing that can happen?"

**Frying chicken in olive oil because you are out of canola:** "What's the worst thing that can happen?"

**Living one more day without accepting Jesus as your Lord and Savior:** "What's the worst thing that can happen?"

I can get past a bad career decision. Getting lost on vacation may actually end up as a funny memory. If the chicken gets ruined, I can always have cereal. These things are insignificant compared to the one decision that has eternal consequences.

A fatal automobile accident is not any anyone's schedule. The massive heart attack is not in your Daytimer. If death comes calling unexpectedly, and you have not committed yourself to Jesus, it's too late. You've got to make the decision now. Your relationship with Jesus must begin while you are here.

Where are you in your walk with Christ? Are you a seeker, a baby Christian or the next great saint? For those of you out there who have never considered God a part of your day-to-day lives, can I ask a favor of you? Will you at least think about it? I mean, you've gotten to the end of this book, so it has to be on your mind, right? Someone or something possessed you to read a book about why we should worship God in this crazy world. Do you think it could have been the subtle work of God in your life? Could it be? Could God care enough about you to want you to

## Finale

know Him better? Absolutely! So please, just think about it. It's a life altering decision for the better. A relationship with God, through Jesus, is the missing puzzle piece in your life; the void you've been trying to fill.

So, that's all I know. May your worship be sizzlin' hot! If you've made it to this final paragraph, I'm assuming you read the whole book (or skipped to the last page). If you have read the whole thing, I would like to thank you for bearing with me. I always welcome feedback—good or bad. Feel free to email me through the "contact us" section of our website, whyworhsipGod.com. In the meantime, I'll see you at church. I'll be easy to find…I'm the guy smiling. God bless!

# Notes

**Introduction**
1. Revelation 3:15-16
2. Exodus 20:8
3. 2 Kings 17:36-39
4. Psalm 150:1-6

**Chapter 1**
1. John 16:33
2. Joshua 24:15
3. Genesis 2:16-17
4. Genesis 3:19
5. Genesis 3:16
6. Ezekiel 28:12
7. Ezekiel 28:15, 17
8. Luke 11:9/Matthew 21:22

**Chapter 2**
1. 1 Philippians 1:6

**Chapter 4**
1. 1 Philippians 4:6

**Chapter 5**
1. Romans 8:24-25
2. Jeremiah 29:11

**Chapter 6**
1. Romans 12:6-8
2. Romans 12:4-6
3. Genesis 2:18
4. Philippians 4:19
5. Romans 13:1

# WHY WORSHIP GOD?

**Chapter 7**
1. Genesis 1:26-30

**Chapter 8**
1. Ecclesiastes 4:4
2. Proverbs 14:30
3. Ecclesiastes 2:7-8, 10-11
4. 1 Timothy 6:7
5. Matthew 5:45
6. Ecclesiastes 8:14
7. Luke 10:27 and Matthew 22:37

**Chapter 9**
1. Philippians 2:6-7
2. Mark 2:18
3. Ephesians 2:8
4. John 3:16
5. Romans 6:23
6. John 19:19
7. John 19:30
8. Matthew 11:28-30
9. John 8:3-6
10. John 8:7-11

**Chapter 10**
1. James 1:2-3
2. James 1:5
3. Ecclesiastes 8:14
4. John 9:3
5. Job 11:16
6. 2 Corinthians 4:17
7. Psalm 23:4
8. 1 Peter 5:7 and Psalm 55:22

# WHY WORSHIP GOD?

**Chapter 11**
1. Matthew 6:25-27
2. Matthew 6:28-34
3. Romans 8:31
4. Romans 8:28
5. John 14:1

**Chapter 12**
1. John 14:2
2. Philippians 3:20
3. 2 Timothy 4:7
4. Revelation 21:1
5. Luke 23:43
6. Luke 13:11
7. Luke 13:16
8. Job 1:11
9. Job 2:7

**Chapter 13**
1. 1 Peter 5:6
2. Hebrews 4:16

# WHY WORSHIP GOD?

**About Matt...**

**Matt Oppenheim** is about as regular of a guy as you can think of. Insurance salesman by day, family man by night, he is a big fan of his girls, college football, grilling, woodworking, and various sports (which he is no good at).

Matt grew up in Meridian, Mississippi, and graduated from the University of Mississippi with a degree in Marketing. After graduating, he moved to Memphis, and began his career in employee benefits sales. In 2001, he met Kim, and they were wed the following year. They now live in a suburb of Memphis with their two girls, and attend Hope Presbyterian Church in Cordova, Tennessee.

www.ingramcontent.com/pod-product-compliance
Lightning Source LLC
Chambersburg PA
CBHW060526100426
42743CB00009B/1440